DUE

To Emma and Judy

Photographing Architecture and Interiors

by Julius Shulman

Introduction by Richard J. Neutra

Whitney Library of Design, New York

Format and Typography: Lou Klein/Phil Gips

Composition: The Composing Room

Printing: Robert Teller Sons & Dorner

Library of Congress Catalog Card No. 62-18473

Text © 1962, Whitney Library of Design

Charles E. Whitney, President

William Wilson Atkin, Vice-President

a division of Whitney Publications, Inc.

18 East 50th Street, New York 22, New York

Publishers of Interiors and Industrial Design

Photographs © 1960 by Julius Shulman

Contents

The Photographer and Architect by Richard J. Neutra

Do we just like beautiful photographs of our buildings?

What makes me happy is a design idea fitting sensitively into the landscape as I may long have carried it with me. Now, suddenly, it appears once again, clearly hinted at least, in a still picture.

One such picture never can give quite all of it. Perhaps a whole series, from every point of view and from every position, might do, but it would have to be repeated whenever daylight and artificial illumination change. But, then, a series simply never is equal to the grand experience of visual continuity.

Architecture is *not* frozen music—it is nothing frozen at all! It plays on us in time, the vivid time of our living responses which melt one moment into the next, and one impression into what follows, while we minutely move the eye, turn and tilt the head, or step through spaces and past forms—all those features of a building the architect has arranged. A photograph, of course, cannot be looked at in so many ways. From the moment it was exposed onto the negative behind the lens, it was "frozen."

The still optics of the camera oppose physiological time optics even in our retinal chemistry. There, sensitivities are in flux, they do not remain static as on a fabricated film. Everything in our reactive life-body changes every second, but everything is rigid on that 8 x 10 print.

Photography can be a heartbreaking job for a man who is called to find his stand before a complicated piece of architecture, accumulated or designed over years. It has been a long, laborious process to arrive at this momentous morning or evening of picture taking. What is the photographer supposed to do when he suddenly, for the first time, lays eyes on this project unless the architect can tell him what design features had really been foremost in his own mind and had been worked into this composition? It is this composition or nothing which must come out strikingly in order to give any satisfaction and make the whole effort worthwhile. If the architect knew only such roughly defined subjects for photography as the main entrance, the elevator lobby, or the master bedroom, and left all the rest of it to the photographer, later merely criticizing the proofs and turning them down, this would make a terribly wasteful process out of the whole backbreaking thing. The architect who has conceived and creatively worked on this composition, and truly has devotion and gifts for it, cannot be a guesser when it comes to photography—there is little time for guessing. It is a breath-taking job while the sun is moving from one shadow cast to another and from one illumination to the next. He will have to know his building by heart as a conductor knows his score; and the time element, as mentioned, plays an important role. Or else the poor photographer is carrying his heavy tripod and a big suitcase of paraphernalia, including floodlights, trailing from the stairhall to the lower grounds and then up to the master bedroom opening onto a terrace, which the whole party reaches about ten minutes after the sun has slipped away from the "right" angle. The architect must know what design features and compositions the whole exploration-and-hunting party is after or else a daily dozen of pictures are all just flops.

Left alone to his own devices on the scene of the "crime," the photographer would have to be a Sherlock Holmes. He has to do a lot of fast thinking when nobody tells him on what portion of that interior, with windows outward, he should quickly use his light meter in order not to get just something or other on the film, but to catch the main point of his shot.

How to connect indoors and outdoors by photography in so-called indoor-outdoor architecture is in itself quite a problem. It concerns the pro and con of which lens to use, and, perhaps, how to make the most impressive trees out there look like insignificant weeds, and to make mountains into molehills; or how to show them well only to find there is no space left on the ground glass for the interior in the foreground to frame the landscape by architecture *as it was thus actually conceived and composed.*

It sounds so simple and means so little to call a camera candid. The camera itself does not know it but a very large number of most promising, well photo-angled shots can be taken which are not only beautiful but which actually show the *design intention.* Then, the photographer's time is not being wasted but many of his shots, done at great speed one after the other, prove useful and gratifyingly emotive. This is what pictorializing has done for us since the pre-historic wall paintings of bisons in the Altamira caves. I guess the artist himself and the photographer would enjoy the work in company with somebody who knows where the ''game'' can be found, at what time of day and at what certain spot, instead of saying, ''Now we missed it again! We should have been here much earlier, or there much later.'' Within exactly the same frame and from precisely the same angle ''it,'' or at least ''something'' of it can be badly missed, or happily accomplished. There is great significance in choosing exposure time. Best examples of this most vital problem of composite registering of values and emotive contrasts, or possibly played down discernability, is a matter of on what do you expose? Is it on the vaultings of the cathedral, the roof purlins of the church, or on its windows, or on the outside beyond the open portal where you see the fantastic cloud over an interestingly shaped tree?

What is the emotive, the stimulative purpose of this picture? I can send a photographer out to get the loftiness of the cathedral nave capped by fantastic structure which has become an architectural symbol of the mystic and deep religious elation. He goes there, sees that lovely cloud over the plaza, and exposes for it instead of the building. It is like sending a photographer to the zoo to photograph an elephant. But he falls in love with the giraffe and brings back a giraffe picture instead.

My beloved late Edward Weston (and I am happy and proud to have launched him with a travelling show from Munich all over Europe when almost no one knew of him) was no architectural photographer! Innocently he fell in love with stunning cracks in buckly plaster. His wonderful photos could have served as evidence in court against a plastering contractor. Architectural photography is an applied art. Architectural photographers like Julius Shulman apply themselves to the art of the befriended architect. They must select, to approximate *essential* memory images.

And photography is *statically* selective while real seeing goes on selecting, of course, most dynamically. It does so through the seconds, the hours of the day—perpetually, from sunrise to sunset. It does not put pictures into numbered files but into mobile, perhaps subconscious, but ever emotive memory treasure. Sometimes a sequence of subsequent moments of vision are linked in a string. At other times sight impressions spaced and separated by long intervals are miraculously fused into one visual memory. Only the start of it happens in the eye; then it plays from the rear lobe all over the brain roof and into the emotional centers of the attic under that roof.

An architect is, among other things, himself an applied artist of physiological optics and, even more so, of its cerebral sequels—its consequences in a stirred-up human soul. It is a soul so much more rich and complicated than that of an animal who cannnot appreciate pictures, that in fundamental religions ''soul'' means simply a unique human property. And a photographer can and does speak to human souls.

Mr. Shulman's first step in the direction of architectural photography was taken while he was studying a liberal arts course in 1936. A friend took him to see a new house in California by Richard J. Neutra and, in the amateur manner, he took snapshots of everything. He had recently acquired an Eastman Vest Pocket Camera and owned an unusual carved wood Japanese enlarger. He sent the 8 x 10 glossies to his friend who showed them to Mr. Neutra.

A lens is chosen not simply to get an interesting shot. It is a battle to simulate wide sweeping living eye impressions as an architect serves and provides for. It is a battle never quite won by the camera, any camera, which attempts it by static means, whereas the two eyes are a team of endlessly dynamic and mobile advantages.

A church nave may lead to an altar wall with one half of it open onto a snowy mountain peak. It is a thrill to behold but photographically that peak becomes a mere unimportant speck on the photo, like the rising moon in a love scene photographed with high-speed film! How can the photographer express my compositional thoughts for the Claremont Church in its landscape anchorage, except perhaps by a series of shots: when parishioners approach the communion rail, the church stands fixed—but the view onto the snowy mountain chain unrolls like a ritual, ever widening to the right, the more they advance to the tall, silhouetted cross. At last now, it looms meaningfully right into the ever-changing universe of grand clouds, the illuminations and shadows of the day's hours and the year's seasons. What can the photographer do about it in one single exposure? He must be happy to hint.

The "indoor-outdoor" architecture, the open air plus interior assembly of worshipers or deeply excited spectators of offered dramatics, all are an inspiring task to the architect but a heartbreak to the photographer who must master this complexity in one vision.

On the other hand, he can easily become a technically sophisticated misguide to "find the right angle," photograph a compositional impossibility, and hit—inmidst inane lack of anticipation which the composer of clashing slants and zigzags, or of perspectively incompatible curves may have shown—on the one hard-to-find, accidental angle that makes it look possible. He may even present it as if it were a prominent and grand intention. Such glorification of architectural accident makes out of a photographer a dramatic actor on his own. With one gesture he may evoke untold illusions.

Simulating a speedy antelope or racehorse with a few pencil lines that stay put on paper has been possible to an artist for 20,000 years. What is really simulated is our inner emotion on seeing the original alive and seeing the picture. We are *only* interested in our human response to both. And so it is with photography. Technically, mechanically, chemically limited, it, naturally, can never be the same as the life object but it can approximate. It can be emotive, simulating perhaps our mood as if we stood still a moment before the design, never quite as if we walked through and around it, to relate a million pictures in one memory.

Also, photoscopic seeing and color photography is not just getting "true" color, but getting us emotional the same way as when we faced the real hues in their context.

One can no more convey the excitement of a heated fight by getting in a snapshot one uppercut of a pugilist than one can photograph in color the illumination of the sky before a sunrise as seen from the master bed through the window, over lake and mountains, in one frozen still. The excitement is that, while the eye accommodates to intensity No. 1, the illumination goes on intensifying to No. 2 and beyond all such figures and grading and mechanics—our emotion in a crescendo (musicians have a word for it) reaches its highest brilliance.

The architect who lovingly lives a multitude of realities ahead of realization, finds afterwards when he wants to remember and commemorate, a wonderful ally in the photographer who feels himself in, and gives what a camera can give.

Julius Shulman is such a friendly companion and has made me, over one quarter of a century, appreciate photographers.

Richard J. Neutra

Architectural photography is the term generally used for the photography of buildings, inside and out. A photographer who specializes in this field is known as an architectural photographer.

Photography has always had two fundamental purposes; sometimes these are quite separate, sometimes they exist together in the same picture. The first is that of creating a picture that is in itself a work of art and not primarily dependent on its subject matter; the elements of this kind of photography closely parallel those of a painting. The second purpose is to convey a message about the subject matter. This message may be one of clarification, simplification, or illustration in which cases the picture is complementing another medium of message-carrying. Alternatively, it may stand alone as the whole message to which any other media used are subordinate. In this second purpose, that of carrying a message, photography is a means of communication and it is with this function that we are primarily concerned here.

As the world grows smaller and the population larger it becomes more and more essential that people and peoples learn to live together amicably. Real amity depends on understanding and to understand you have to know. It is consequently essential that communications be complete and unambiguous. Communications is the key to awareness and understanding and as such can help to relieve tensions between neighbors, individuals and nations alike.

It is in this respect that photography can (and largely has) come into its own because the visual message is probably the most quickly and clearly understood of any and its impact is sharp enough to attract attention to the information it carries. It is surely true that photographic coverage of an event can convey more about it to more people than any number of words.

There are as many subjects for photography as there are kinds of photographs but we are here concerned with one particular subject: the design of buildings; i.e. architecture and interior design. As a part of our environment the design of buildings is of paramount importance. It affects the lives of all people at all times, physically, psychologically, and sociologically. The task of conveying the facts of their existence, meaning, and importance is rapidly devolving on photography which performs this function in several ways. It enhances awareness of an already-familiar environment. It prepares for the actual experience of being at or in a building. It substitutes for that experience until it occurs, if it ever does. And it "freezes" the design, thus providing a

Seen a thousand times in publications, Lever House in New York always offers possibilities for new and striking composition. Here a column of the Seagram Building on the other side of Park Avenue has been borrowed for scale and impact. Note how the dynamic shadow line responds to that of the tree branch. Lever House, New York, N.Y. Skidmore, Owings & Merrill, Architects.

1

Taliesen West, Scottsdale, Arizona. Frank Lloyd Wright, Architect.

quality of experience never to be found in being in the building itself.

The impact of architectural photography is just as great and no less useful as that of any other kind. A United Nations committee working with local groups in the Congo on educational facilities can convey more with ten photographs of Western school buildings and layout than it could with the proverbial 10,000 words.

The photographer (and here we are talking of the man taking the photograph, whether he is a professional photographer or no) must approach his task with understanding and sympathy for the design professions. Not only for the ones with which he is most directly concerned—architecture and interiors—but also for industrial design, graphic design, landscape architecture, and engineering design. He must also be prepared to subjugate his photograph to the design. A photographer must remember that he is not doing a class exercise in artistic photography; he is performing the difficult and serious task of re-creating on a two-dimensional piece of paper the intrinsic qualities of a three-dimensional design. His job is particularly serious if he is a professional architectural photographer because not only is he recording an already whole work of art, but his portrayal of a building will produce an image of that building in the public's mind. If his representation is a sensitive one it will hasten the process of evaluating good design in relation to environment. If he is not a professional architectural photographer, he must bear in mind at all times the purpose of photographing

design as such and not wander off into the (siren) regions of art photography. This is not to say that there is no place for the art photograph within the architectural milieu. This kind of photograph can be so compelling in itself that it will capture the reader's attention and direct it to the essential design features of a building. However, remembering that the purpose of architectural photography is to convey information about the design, one should beware of the photograph which calls too much attention to its own art, thereby detracting from the art of its subject matter. Such a photograph is not truly a work of art for it can fail in its purpose.

In his book "Looking into Art," Frank Seiberling, Chairman of the Department of Art at the University of Iowa describes one effect of music as "invoking a wide range of feelings." In many ways a photograph of a building can be similarly compared in its effect upon the viewer's attitude toward architecture.

Although architectural photography can be defined as a physical recording of the image of design, the photographer can develop an ability to transcend the mere physical recording. The photograph can then become instrumental in evoking empathy with the design. It is also true that experience in taking architectural photographs will expand the technical abilities and the appreciation of the person taking the photographs until eventually, with application, there will evolve a freedom and creativity of expression that will make the photograph a work of art in its own right.

The architect and the interior designer would do well to

Emphasis of form and materials is one of the best ways to enhance the dynamic force of industrial structures. Note the effect of back lighting on the black tile. Texture and life-like brilliance would have been lost had the photograph been taken earlier in the day with flatter lighting. General Dynamics Astronautics, San Diego, California. Charles Luckman Associates, William L. Pereira Associates, Architects.

The essence of a design can be expressed by selecting the major theme and in the choice of lighting and film. Here a strong curve has been used to convey circular form and the rectangular mass in background to provide dimensional quality. Infrared film gives sharp delineation. Parke-Davis Building, Pico-Rivera, California. Charles Luckman Associates, Architects.

acquire some knowledge of the craft of architectural photography whether or not he ever has or ever will hold a camera in his own two hands.

Since photography is nowadays the main link between the designer and his public, it is essential that the former have some voice about what aspects of his design are presented to the latter and in what form. This is only possible if he knows what photography and the photographer are about. No photographer can be expected to fathom the mind of a designer so profoundly that he can transfer the results of years of planning onto film without any guidance as to the essential aspects of the design. Nor, on the other hand, can the photographer be expected to take directives from a designer who has not the slightest grasp of the photographic medium. Therefore, the designer should have a working knowledge of photography so that he will neither expect miracles from his photographer nor put up with inferior work out of sheer ignorance.

With a knowledgeable clientele to work for it is quite probable, too, that the standard of professional architectural photography could be uniformly raised. Not only would the photographer find that below-par work would be recognized and rejected but, with an articulate designer who could discuss photography intelligently, his own insights into design might be more easily and truly developed.

A third advantage of a working knowledge of photography accrues to the student designer in particular and to all designers—and we trust for design's sake that they are many—who still feel that they have something to learn about design. If a designer knows how photographs are composed he will learn to analyze more critically the photographs that he sees of his own and others' work. He will also learn, through the camera eye, many things about his own craft. For example, an element that may have seemed minor in the design concept can be thrown into startling prominence by the camera eye and this in turn may lead to a whole new train of ideas in the designer's mind. Again, photography is an excellent means of exploring and recording for future reference whatever aspects of a design are intriguing or puzzling or just worthwhile.

We are not recommending that every designer become his own photographer—he will have neither the time nor, probably, the inclination for such specialization as would make him competent for the rôle. However, we *do* recommend that every designer have a working knowledge of photographic processes.

So far as photography (as well as many other things) is concerned, architecture and interiors are well-nigh inseparable. They have only been divided in this book where clarity of discussion so demands.

Awareness of scale and form helps to create photographs with impact. Wayfarers' Chapel, Palos Verdes, California. Lloyd Wright, Architect.

Before embarking on the methods of photography, let us explore the uses of the architectural photograph of professional status. Of the widely varied uses those which are primarily concerned with the professional (architectural) photographer's business are discussed in Chapter V. Here we are concerned with their use to the architect and interior designer. Let us stress that in this chapter we are talking, not of the designer's or amateur's own pictures, but of those taken for him by a professional photographer as a permanent, and probably public, record of his work. The selection of a good photographer is important. No designer would dream of employing inferior craftsmen on the building itself; his feeling for his work should extend to its photography. The difference between a bargain photographic coverage and an expensive one is often not very great; it is hardly worth the risk of loss of quality even in monetary terms. And, to coin a phrase, the result is often flivver photography for a Rolls Royce quality building.

The question of fees and use rights is dealt with fully in Chapter VI but basically there are two types of each. The fee may be paid outright for a certain number of photographs or it may be paid on the basis of time spent on the project. Use rights may be purchased in full or limited use rights may be bought with residual rights remaining with the photographer; the fee for the limited rights is, naturally, less than for full rights.

File Record

A portable file in which their important work is represented by prints at least 8 x 10 in size is valuable to all architects and interior designers. These can be assembled by one of the numerous methods on the market utilizing ready-made spiral and plastic binders. It is wise to use uniform binders so that, eventually, a library of work can be assembled with each job in its own separate folder. Someone in the office should be made responsible for maintaining an up-to-date file so that photographs are readily available at all times.

Job Presentation

Many a job is clinched by dramatic presentation and a set of attractive prints can aid in making such a presentation. There are architects who feel that photographic records (particularly of domestic work) are unnecessary and that all one has to do is hop in the car and drive over to the building itself. Apart from the obvious inconvenience that may be caused by distance, driving conditions, etc., the architect and his prospective client might run into an awkward situation at their

Photographs of "antique" design work can offer informative background material on architectural history. Bradbury Building (1892) Los Angeles, California. George Herbert Wyman, Architect.

*A pegboard in an architect's office is ideal
for hanging display photographs
since size and spacing of the photographs
can be varied at will. Note the continuous
light fixture which produces even
illumination on the wall. Office, Palm
Springs, California. Williams & Williams,
Architects.*

destination. It can, for instance, be most embarrassing to drop in on a friendly owner and find the place in an uproar with last night's dishes strewn around the kitchen, clothing on every chair in the house, and the bathroom full of toothpaste. On the other hand it is very convenient for the architect to be able to hand his prospective client a set of photographs without a drapery fold displaced, with flower arrangements in the living room, a warm inviting fire in the fireplace, and with landscaping, perhaps, transformed from sparse and seedy to lush and blooming with full-grown trees framing the structure.

In non-domestic work there is usually little doubt of the need for photographs. An architect, for example, due to make a presentation before a school board certainly cannot go unarmed into the fray. His ammunition of facts, figures, and photographs must be sufficient for presentation in as complete a form as possible. The format of presentation is, naturally, up to the individual architect and he can have single 8 x 10 prints or huge blow-ups, ten photographs or a hundred.

Office Exhibit

Even the most drab and miniscule office space can be made attractive with a carefully thought-out exhibit and photographs can be an important part of the display. Such an exhibit should be arranged in relationship to the wall size and to the subject matter. So far as photographs are concerned it is advisable to avoid the use of 8 x 10 glossies for display purposes; the most successful display prints are those that can be readily observed from several feet away for the scale of such prints produces a more realistic quality. Optimum sizes range from 11″ x 14″ to 16″ x 20″, even larger if space permits. The photographs should not remain on the wall so long as to become fly-specked and dusty—a state almost as bad as no exhibition at all. In addition, the illustration of work done two, five, or ten years ago is hardly fair to a designer whose work might be expected to be progressing (or at least, changing) in terms of concept and maturity. Office exhibitions should therefore be kept up-to-date, both for the sake of appearance and to show current work.

Public Exhibit

A third use for the architectural photograph is in public exhibitions. One particularly effective place for exhibition is in building lobbies or offices of organizations related to the design and building trades and industries. Architects and interior designers would be well advised to have a circulating exhibition of their work among banks, building and loan associations, material and equipment manufacturers, and other institutions and organizations which constantly are on the look-out for display materials. In some cases the local chapters of the American Institute of Architects, the

Residence ("Prairie Chicken"), Norman, Oklahoma. Herb Greene, Architect.

Photographic displays of architecture are often used for public exhibition in such places as museums, lobbies, and lecture halls. This is an exhibition of the work of Richard J. Neutra at the University of California at Los Angeles (UCLA).

American Institute of Interior Designers, and the National Society of Interior Designers conduct this kind of program and see to it through their exhibit chairmen that a representation of their members' work is constantly before the public's eye.

In addition, there are, of course, gallery and museum exhibits, usually when a special show is being done. Some of these are travelling exhibits and are consequently useful for getting the designer's name before the public throughout the country. Travelling exhibits are mostly sponsored by church guilds, hospital associations, school and educational groups, manufacturers' associations, and photographers' associations. The exhibits are often the results of competitions. As they are well publicized and shown in many cities, it is well worth the designer's effort to participate in as many as possible. Since announcements of exhibits and competitions are usually sent out well in advance, designers might profitably use the time to select material and prepare their exhibits carefully. The photographer, with his knowledge of graphic presentation, can often help with this. Several national museums hold exhibits of more than ordinary value. The Museum of Modern Art, in particular, has arranged many exhibits of great educational value.

Publication

At present, perhaps the most valuable use of photography to the architect or interior designer is its publication in magazines and books devoted to the presentation of architectural information or to those aspects of it which are considered to be of interest to the general public. Hundreds of publications throughout the world seek to present to their readers outstanding design news. The field is so extensive that no one architect or designer can expect to do much more than make a small dent in it. Realizing that publication of his work represents the finest public relations he can achieve, the designer will see to it that his work is constantly presented to editors. Although acceptance for publication is not the simplest matter to arrange, the designer should work at it in an efficient and organized fashion. A photographer's own relationship and commitments with magazines can, of course, assist the architect in getting his work published.

Much to the surprise of many people, the editor sitting at his desk in New York, Des Moines, or wherever he happens to reside, is a relatively humane person. He has only one head and two hands and is generally trying to do a good job of rounding up the best possible material to fill the needs of his publication. Editors receive literally tons of mail every year and they are obliged to go through every piece of it. It seems obvious that in view of this anyone who wished to get a job published should investigate the magazine thoroughly before submitting his work. This, unfortunately, is not what happens; the bulk of material submitted to a magazine is practically useless and very often simply because it has gone to the wrong magazine. There is also, of course, a question of quality that enters here. Many designers (and photographers) read into their work an originality of concept and beauty of realization that simply do not exist and are therefore continually disappointed that editors are not knocked off their chairs by the submissions.

To establish a working program for submitting material to magazines, photographers and designers should analyze the market carefully to understand just what it is about their design that will appeal to a particular editorial policy. The initial contact with a magazine seems to many architects, interior designers, and photographers a mysterious and difficult project. In point of fact, editors almost invariably welcome designers and photographers and give their work the utmost consideration. It is always wise to write to an editor before sending in a project for his inspection. It is pointless, for instance, to send in a new library job to a magazine which has just completed an issue on libraries or never touches the subject. It saves much time and trouble if the general acceptability of a work is confirmed in advance.

This having been settled, the designer (or photographer) can submit photographs of his work to the magazine for evaluation. If the magazine is interested it may commission one of its editors and a photographer to make a complete coverage. If the architect submits material on a project, then the magazine is likely to wait until near completion of the work before making such a coverage unless they decide to publish it as a project in which case model photographs may be required.

When a designer or photographer submits work for publication, he should do it ethically: he should not, that is, submit to several magazines at once, particularly to several competitive magazines. On the other hand, he may be able to arrange for publication of one work in several magazines which are interested in different aspects of design or who are in no sense competitive. But in any case he should be perfectly frank with each about his other submissions and any acceptances.

It is wise to establish a check list of all magazines that may at one time or another have publication possibilities. This should cover two aspects: the type of photograph that the magazines are prone to use; and the type of work in which they are interested. So far as the type of photograph is concerned, some publications prefer snapshot or candid photographs, some prefer more formal and studied compositions; some prefer the presence of animated interest such as people or animals; others consider this a distraction from the design elements. These are rarely hard and fast rules with any magazine but it is useful to know about general preferences so that job after job will not be turned down purely on the grounds of photographic composition.

The type of work in which a magazine is interested is most easily ascertained by study of a number of recent issues. Besides the architectural magazines, there are the home magazines, some general consumption magazines, and technical and trade journals.

What follows is a general review of the field of magazine publications in the United States of America and their characteristics. The greatest demand for photographs of residences comes from magazines that publish low- or medium-cost single family dwellings, or individual design or decorating ideas from houses and apartments. These include popular home and general magazines, such as *American Home, Better Homes and Gardens, Good Housekeeping, Ladies' Home Journal,* and *McCall's.* Some of these magazines have editorial representatives in various parts of the country who make it their business to contact architects, designers, and photographers regularly so that they can keep up-to-date with work being done. Most of them, on locating a house with good story possibilities, work directly with the photographer and pay all expenses and assignment fees so that the architect or interior designer is in no way financially involved. These magazines provide excellent publicity outlets with circulations running into the millions, a large percentage of which consist of home builders or other potential architectural or interior design clients.

Magazines such as *House & Garden* and *House Beautiful* generally publish houses of different types. Their overall emphasis is on houses somewhat more expensive in the quality of their interior design and of larger square footage. However, they do not neglect the small home entirely and often will devote extensive space to small houses that have unusual solutions to site, plan, or design problems in general.

Almost all garden editors of home service magazines are constantly seeking material on landscaping, outdoor living areas, terraces, patios, and other such features and the market for material of this type is a good one.

Many general magazines publish residential and non-residential architecture. *Life* magazine occasionally features unusual and often startling architecture. The publication of architectural subjects in a mass magazine of this kind aids considerably in presenting to the public many facets of the world of design. *Life* will consider all the work presented by photographers but it is advisable that photographers present only work of dynamic and unusual design and photographic quality.

Holiday magazine features vacation houses and unique treatment of dining (indoors and out), bathrooms, kitchens, and lighting installations in all houses.

Look magazine occasionally presents thorough and objective analyses presenting architectural news with superlative photography. Many newspapers, particularly in their Sunday or week-end issues, run design stories. The real estate sections are usually concerned with new domestic and commercial structures and the Sunday magazine sections will often carry stories on residential design and occasionally on modern architecture. *The Los Angeles Times Home Magazine* supplement contains, week after week throughout the year, presentations of landscaping, architecture, and interiors. It publishes special features on swimming pools, kitchens, bathrooms, terraces, and other specific areas including arts and crafts in the home. This magazine not only gives solid information to its readers but also attracts profitable advertising from building material companies and other organizations providing services to the home owner.

Publication of his residential work in a magazine is unlikely to mean that an architect or interior designer will be swamped with calls, letters, and telegrams from all parts of the country. It is more likely that few queries will be received as a direct result of the publication. It has, of course, been known for a client to materialize from among the magazine readers. Nor are such clients always from magazines which have given a full presentation of a job. For instance, only a kitchen may have been featured in an issue devoted to this subject. While this may not have seemed a particularly important matter to the designer at the time, commissions for whole jobs have been known to result from just this kind of presentation. The true function of this kind of publicity, of

The image of the research institution is changing and environment and facilities, properly illustrated, can be used to attract new staff members. Infrared film used for the two exteriors has detailed recording of the setting. Hoffman Science Center, Santa Barbara, California. William L. Pereira Associates, Architects.

course, is an educative one, long term in its results. Continual publication of good domestic architecture raises its general standards; thus it will be seen that the architect or interior designer who has something to offer succeeds where others may fail.

Architects and interior designers who specialize in home design should, therefore, always be conscious of the long-term value of getting material published.

The previous paragraphs have discussed general magazines which tend to emphasize residential architecture and design. Although these reach a great mass market, there are as many, if not more, publications whose policy is the opposite and which feature non-residential design. The audience for this latter type of publication is apt to be more professional and, although in sheer numbers residential architecture has greater volume, in terms of building dollars non-residential architecture far outweighs it.

First, there are the professional architectural and design magazines. In general they publish anything to do with the professional field, but there are nuances of emphasis which it is good to know about.

The major nationally distributed magazines devoted to news of the architectural world in this country are *Architectural Forum, Architectural Record, House & Home, Interiors,* and *Progressive Architecture.* The *Journal of the American Institute of Architects* also presents architects' work and many A.I.A. chapters have publications of their own some of which use pictorial matter.

There are also some magazines of a smaller circulation which have impact on design progress. *Arts and Architecture* and *Landscape* are examples of this kind of magazine. In addition there are three magazines which are published for the home builder: *American Builder, Practical Builder,* and the *Journal of the National Association of Home Builders.* All the architectural magazines, with the exception of the *Architectural Forum,* which carries only non-residential material, publish residential,* as well as all types of commercial and public buildings. They offer excellent opportunities for publicity for the architect or designer. *Architectural Forum* often uses so-called action views of buildings. The editors often intersperse straightforward architectural pictures with detailed photographs of activities in the building.

In addition to the architectural journals there are magazines which cover each kind of non-residential architecture.

*House & Home, published by Time, Inc. who also publish *Architectural Forum,* publishes only homes.

For example, there are numerous church publications. Each denomination publishes journals whose editors are interested in showing buildings. There are also magazines devoted to offices, hospitals, schools, libraries, and virtually every other type of building.

Besides America, almost every country in the world publishes architectural magazines, some of which are of exceptionally high standard. To be published in Italy's *Domus*, for example, is to have one's work shown in one of the world's outstanding design publications. The prestige and public relations value is of great significance for European magazines are widely distributed in this country. Amongst those worth noting are: *Architectural Design*, England; *Architectural Review*, England; *L'Architecture d'Aujourd'hui*, France; *Arquitectura Mexico*; *The Canadian Architect*; *Kenchiku Bunka*, Japan; *Ons Huis*, Holland; and *Techniques et Architecture*, France.

The foregoing description of publications has stressed

architectural and the more popular magazines; scores of other magazines represent other design professions.

Interior work is represented in numerous local magazines in various parts of the country. These emphasize decoration and are generally read by decorators and interior designers.

Book publication is another important outlet for the architectural photograph. Requests for pictures usually come from the author (rather than the publisher who is not, as a rule, contractually concerned) to the architect or interior designer. Photographic rights are dealt with in detail in Chapter V but a word of warning—the designer should take care that his book rights to the photograph are cleared before handing them over to the usually vague book author. The photographic charge on book rights is generally low but its existence is quite definite and the author should be warned.

Throughout the country boards and building committees, representing every conceivable organization and institution, meet to decide upon new and extended building programs. These boards and committees study publications of the architectural profession as well as those of their immediate establishment which could be a church, a school, an industrial complex, or a neighborhood bank or library. What they see in the publications very greatly effects their decisions.

Institutional Reference

All organizations and institutions whose function is physically associated with design, planning and construction can utilize photography as part of their study program when new or expanded facilities are proposed. A school board, for example, could have a complete file of photographs of all the schools in its district. What more vivid graphic planning preparation for expanding a campus than an aerial photograph? With a clear grasp of the geography of a campus, how much easier and more constructive would be the architectural conference.

Institutional Promotion

Private schools and institutions of higher learning would find that the inclusion of outstanding photographs of facilities in brochures and circulars aids materially in presenting information on the campus to new students and faculty. This applies to other institutions as well. Hospitals, for instance, could use illustrated brochures for distribution to schools of medicine or nursing. Research plants in their search for technicians and scientists could use appealing and informative illustrations depicting the facilities and environment of the organization. Administrators of new facilities in all cate-

gories should collaborate with their architects in presenting material for publication in professional journals so that improvements and new achievements in design and equipment can be widely shown.

Educational

The education of an architect or interior designer is as important to society as that of a doctor, a lawyer, or an engineer. It is therefore the responsibility of our educational institutions to help make this man the greatest designer in the world—at least one of the greatest. Educational methods vary widely. Some schools attract students who admire the precepts of the faculty. In other cases perhaps the architecture practiced by the dean has great appeal. On the other hand, some students prefer schools which do not try to direct or influence their students, attempting instead to keep their students' thinking free from outside influence. Such schools encourage expression with no holds barred! Regardless of the teaching, photography plays a vital role in it. The photograph, most often in the form of a slide, provides a link between the outside world and the workshop or lecture hall. Many architectural and design schools organize their visual programs with particular attention to their collection of 35mm or 2¼″ x 2¼″ color slides. Schools of arts and graphics also study design in its various ramifications and in all of them the use of photographs is prevalent. At the time of writing perhaps the most complete collection of 35mm design material is at Sandak, Inc. of New York who have done a fine assembly job with the aid of a Carnegie grant.

Students on field trips should become proficient in using a camera. It can be their personal instrument of investigation.

One other, almost implicit, use of the architectural photograph to the architect is for revaluation of his own work. The evidence of false fronts, superficial design adaptation, and wholesale plagiarism of design ideas facing us at every turn we take on a street make it obvious that some restudy would be useful.

A little time spent studying the photographs, models, renderings, plans, etc. of one's completed work will often result in a fresh diagnosis of one's design concepts and their workability. We might even venture to suggest that the designer who is willing to accompany his photographer, at least on the latter's first trip to the job, is only showing a proper interest in his own work: both in having it correctly photographed and in seeing it in use after having lived so long with it during design and construction periods.

Architectural landmarks provide excellent study material for students. Photographic studies are essential, especially with the constant danger of demolition in the name of "progress." Christian Science Church, Berkeley California. Bernard Maybeck, Architect.

In this chapter we will describe the basic tools of photography. These descriptions are not intended as a basic instruction course in photography but merely as a general guide, first for the amateur photographer who may have used nothing more complex than a box camera before and then, as the information grows more complex, for the person who wishes to take professional photographs of architecture and interior design.

Initially it should be clearly understood that it is possible to take photographs of architecture and interiors with any type of camera. It is really up to the photographer, as it is up to any craftsman, to decide which are the best tools for him to work with and how best to manipulate them. However, this kind of decision can only be made on the basis of experience and the beginner needs to know where to start. What follows is a description of equipment in general use which has been found to produce good results under the most varied conditions (some of these variations being in the photographer himself). Architectural photography is not particularly complex technically but it will help the beginner to know what is most likely to be the proper tool for any situation.

The Camera

What is a camera? It is nothing but a light-proof box containing light sensitized film and equipped with an aperture through which light can be introduced in the proper quantities to cause an image on the film. In the old days handbooks for boys always included instructions for making a pinhole camera, the pinhole being the aperture which, because of its small size, acted as a lens.

Perhaps the most widely used camera in the world today is the 35mm camera, so-called because it takes a roll film 35mm wide (about 1½″). Its popularity can be largely attributed to its ease of operation, compactness, and particularly facility in color photography. (The film with proper development becomes a color slide.) The 35mm is probably the best camera for capturing spontaneous action and has the added advantage of working well under many lighting conditions, from bright sunlight to deep shade out-of-doors and from bright artificial lights to soft illumination indoors.

Its great drawback for architectural photography is its lack of movement: it cannot be swung or tilted to any large degree and is therefore apt to give a distorted image unless the camera is held perfectly horizontal.

A strong and positive perspective in a design has here been emphasized with a wide angle view of the inter-relationship of areas. Note the great depth of field. Residence, Los Angeles, California. Raphael S. Soriano, Architect.

35mm black and white negatives, if developed carefully, can produce 8 x 10 prints sufficiently sharp and brilliant for reproduction on the printed page. For the amateur their disadvantage lies in the difficulty of viewing the results of the shots taken. It is costly to have large positives made from every negative used; the answer is what is called the contact strip—a series of small frames, exactly the same size as professional movie frames, printed in strips or in takes on a sheet of photographic printing paper. Those required for enlargement may be marked accordingly for processing.

Until recently the 35mm color transparency was considered suitable for projection and for a color record of subjects taken in black and white with a larger camera, but not for enlargement or reproduction. However, engraving and printing processes, as well as film itself, have so improved recently that it is becoming perfectly feasible to use transparencies for these latter purposes. The writer, in the publication of some pictures in *Life*, had color photographs used that were taken with 4 x 5 and 35mm camera sizes. It was impossible to differentiate between the two as published in the magazine.

As a result of its popularity there is a wide range of accessories available for the 35mm camera. The most important feature for the architectural photographer is the interchangeable lens. The whole matter of lenses is discussed in detail following this discussion of cameras, at this stage suffice it to say that the type and size of lens used controls the depth and coverage of field by the camera.

The 35mm camera's standard lens, which is of 50mm focal length, while good for informal and some detail photography, is too narrow in angle to get entire rooms or buildings on one shot at a reasonable distance. Therefore it is essential, even if more expensive, to get an interchangeable lens camera.

Many 35mm interchangeable lens cameras are available. Some old stand-bys which have been on the market for years are still amongst the finest cameras made: for instance, the Leica and the Contax. Another fine and very dependable camera, high priced in this class, is the Minolta which comes equipped with an f/1.8, 55mm standard lens; a 28mm wide angle lens fitting is available. Another quality interchangeable lens camera, the Pentax, not quite so expensive will take a 28mm wide angle lens, too. Even higher are the Nikon and the Canon—also very fine 35mm cameras. The wide angle lens for these cameras should be no narrower than 28mm or coverage will not be adequate. Nor should it be wider than

24mm; 21mm covers a full 90° but the risks of distortion with just a slight tilting of the camera are very great and, for average use, not worth the trouble.

For the budding photographer, amateur and professional alike, the standard lens with which the 35mm camera is already equipped on purchase plus an interchangeable wide angle lens are excellent starters. Later, a narrow lens, perhaps 85mm or even 135mm, can be obtained for detail photography.

Another very desirable feature is the range finder which is the best device for focusing a hand camera and is built into most of them. Its operative principle is a simple optic one: the angle of convergence of two beams of light from the subject is measured; the beams are apart at the camera by a distance equal to that between the two apertures of the range finder. By a system of a moving prism or mirror the two beams are aligned while viewing through the eyepiece. Since rangefinders are coupled to the lens of the camera, the point of convergence indicates that the light from the image is in focus and the camera is ready for the sharpest photograph.

The actual image or indicator device within the rangefinder varies according to the type of system used by the manufacturer but the principle remains the same for all cameras. It is easy to learn to operate and the result is a sharpness, particularly at critical distances and with wide lens openings, that is positive and foolproof. By studying compositions through such a mechanism the amateur soon learns that the foreground, middleground, and background of a scene can never all be completely in focus at the same time with the lens at full opening.

A triggering mechanism for moving the film in the camera and thus preventing double exposures is nowadays built-in to all hand cameras. However, it was not a feature of many cameras 10 years ago so that second-hand cameras should be checked for this device—it is invaluable. Nearly all 35mm cameras have mounts for flash attachments. Today, 35mm cameras also may be used on a tripod, of course, and they are practically foolproof as far as loading and unloading is concerned.

To free himself from mechanical and physical problems and to allow maximum expression of architectural interpretation, the photographer must use the camera which will (a) produce a good negative in black and white and a color transparency of adequate size for publication uses; (b) achieve good depth of focus; and (c) cover the largest visual area possible with the minimum amount of distortion either horizontal or vertical. Although the 35mm can be and is used for architectural photography, the most frequently used sizes of camera are those that provide photographic negatives or color transparencies either 4 x 5 or 8 x 10 in size.

There are several other camera sizes which are perfectly adequate for most photographic design work although, since they lack many of the advantages of the 4 x 5 view camera, they have largely fallen into disuse professionally. These are the 2¼ x 3¼ negative-size cameras and the once-popular 3¼ x 4¼. Their greatest difficulty lies in having to study the composition on a ground glass the size of this small negative whereas the ground glass of the 4 x 5 view camera is large enough to make detailed study of the composition possible. In addition, structure, interior and exterior, seems to compose better on a 4 x 5 proportion. Simple arithmetic shows that this is the same as the 8 x 10. Therefore, in composing a scene on the ground glass the photographer is wise to fill the glass with his composition. Not only is this good practice from a technical point of view but also, on making the 8 x 10 enlargements, the full negative is used for the print. The study of the scene on the ground glass is one of the creative methods of photography. It avoids careless composition and develops an eye for objective analysis. Perhaps this is why the old Graflex cameras were so popular and effective, even for action photographs. The photographer literally lived the scene and could register it with complete control because he could trip his shutter at the desired moment. The automatic action of the trigger caused the mirror, which reflected the scene onto the ground glass, to flip aside. This allowed the light from the lens to reach the film. However, since the standard size of print for reproduction is 8 x 10, the 5 x 7 negative is not really suitable if fully composed. Too much cropping is required to get the 8 x 10 proportion.

Before going into the details of the 4 x 5 camera, which is the most important and frequently used camera size for professional architectural work, it would be as well to discuss the use of the 2¼ x 2¼ which, although a small camera, is of great professional use. The small negative is often a life saver. As long as the characteristics and operation of this camera are understood a good 8 x 10 print can be had from it under normal conditions. For instance, in working for publications it may be desirable to demonstrate a structure at work. This may be a series of candid camera type photo-

This exterior was taken from under an umbrella in the rain. The camera was a 2¼ x 2¼ Superwide Hasselblad on a tripod with Kodak Verichrome Pan film. The camera and equipment were chosen for their light weight and compactness, both essential on travelling assignments like this one in the Telemark countryside of Norway. Courtesy of The New York Times.

graphs taken with a hand-held twin-lens Rollei-type camera or with one of the single lens 2¼ x 2¼ cameras of the Hasselblad type. With fast film it is possible, even in color, to work with existing high-level illumination. There are a few brands of 2¼ x 2¼ camera available with wide angle lenses, making it possible to avoid "tight" or narrow scenes and enabling the photographer to present an architectural composition of related areas and masses. One type of 2¼ x 2¼ camera, the Hasselblad, which is equipped with a removable back for roll film and can also take sheet film. The back can be removed complete with the roll of film being used and replaced by another, similar, roll (perhaps color as opposed to black and white) or by sheet film.

However, generally speaking, the small negative camera lacks versatility. Although it is possible to achieve excellent photographs for reproduction from it, it must be realized that because of the lack of controls and movement the photographs will not be suitable for large architectural and design exhibit prints. Furthermore, if they are taken in natural or existing light they are often inferior to the more controlled contrast and general over-all quality of a photograph taken with supplementary lighting and larger film-size camera.

The pictures of the house in Norway were taken for *The New York Times* in a remote area of the picturesque Telemark countryside. A Hasselblad hand camera was the only equipment used for black and white work on this as well as other assignments in Denmark and Germany during the trip. The delivered sets of black and white prints reproduced as sharply as any on the same magazine pages taken with larger cameras; notice also the quality of the picture on page 25 from a Hasselblad negative. Because it has a level on it, this camera can be hand held in places where a tripod could not be set up and where fairly fast shutter speeds are required.

The 4 x 5 and the 8 x 10 are the cameras commonly indicated by the term "view camera." For focusing and composing with these cameras the scene is viewed through a ground glass (which is the same size as the negative) on the back; both take sheet film which is loaded into filmholders. These slide into the camera in a plane exactly in line with the position of the ground glass.

The view camera has many controls and adjustments to varying situations. Its back and front elements can be moved independently of one another. The back can be swung on a horizontal (and vertical) axis to rectify perspective distortion or achieve depth of field. The lens can be tilted on a horizontal (or vertical) axis for sharp focus. The front can be raised or dropped or moved sideways to get the lens and film in the correct relationship when the subject is not on the same plane as the camera.

The 4 x 5 camera is undoubtedly the best one for use in design work. Its negative size is versatile and, with careful exposure and development, this size is useful for contact prints for reference purposes as well as being capable of extreme enlargement. The 4 x 5 color transparency is completely satisfactory to most editors and designers and both it and the 4 x 5 black and white reproduce well on the printed page. The 4 x 5 camera achieves a greater depth of field than 8 x 10 cameras with proportionate focal length lenses.

The 8 x 10 is the other camera size most generally associated with architectural photography. The negative proportion, like the 4 x 5, is good for design compositions and the size of the contact print was at one time regarded as the only one for clarity of reproduction in magazines and books as well as for viewing purposes.

The 8 x 10 is rapidly losing its popularity, however, since most of its virtues are duplicated in the 4 x 5 while most of its vices are not. It is, on a comparative basis, heavier and more awkward in handling and lacking in maneuverability in the tight spots such as small rooms and precipitous rooftops so frequently encountered by our intrepid architectural photographer. Having a longer focal length than the 4 x 5, it also compares unfavorably with it in depth of focus. In addition—and crowning factor—the 8 x 10 film is more expensive and its processing and enlargement more difficult.

Nevertheless, 8 x 10 color transparencies are still requested by a few publications and advertising agencies. If the photographer finds it necessary to own an 8 x 10 camera, the convertible Swiss-made Sinar is probably the best on the market. It has easily interchangeable backs and lenses permitting quick transition from 4 x 5 to 8 x 10.

The selection of a camera, obviously, should be made only after a thorough analysis of individual needs, and careful survey as well as much experience is necessary before choosing a professional model. Above all, it must be clearly understood that the camera is at best an interpretive tool. Each photographer must make his own decision and then learn to use his camera to its fullest potential.

The Lens

Photographers have at their disposal scores of lenses, each of which is made to perform a specific optical function. A building can be made to look fat or thin, squat or long; in fact there is little that cannot be done with the lens. The

Two views of the Sinar in the same extreme position of adjustment for corrections. The camera is tilted upwards to gain more height on the building. The front and back standards are then swivelled to restore verticality. Notice the levels on all the elements of the camera; they help considerably in speedy adjustment. The back is swung to approximate a line parallel with the horizontal front of the building in order to minimize a diminishing perspective and restore it to a more natural appearance. The front lens standard is also swung to a line almost parallel with the back so that, when viewing through the ground glass, depth of focus can be increased.

The Sinar again. Here the 4 x 5 back has been replaced by an 8 x 10 bellows and back. The front lens standard remains but the lens has been changed for one to cover the 8 x 10 film. The bellows shown is a standard one for normal lenses. A bag type one similar to that on the 4 x 5 camera on the previous page is used when wide angle work is done.

photographer should learn the elementary principles of optics. What is a lens? How does it transmit the image so faithfully? What knowledge is necessary for full use of the vast range of types of lenses available?

A lens in its most basic form is usually a piece of glass with its sides ground into convex curves. The purpose of a lens is to bring rays of light from an object into focus upon a piece of film. This can be simply demonstrated by holding a reading glass (which is actually a basic lens) up to a light source. By holding a piece of paper close to the glass and moving it back and forth a point will be found at which the light rays will be pin-pointed on the paper. We have all had the experience of getting burned from the rays of the sun so gathered and concentrated through a magnifying glass. Similarly, the rays of light coming from every point on a subject are transmitted through the lens glass and when the paper or, in the case of the camera, the film, is brought to the "burning" point the lens is said to be in focus. The degree of sharpness and clarity of this image depends upon the quality and construction of the lens. This can range from the basic or reading glass type which was used in the elementary box camera to the complex multi-element lenses for advanced cameras and research work.

Because a lens' focus point is governed by its focal length it is necessary to understand how this is determined and how the photographer applies it in his selection of a lens. We have found that rays of light taken through a lens from a point on the subject converge on the film to form an image of the point. The distance of this point from the center of the lens is the focal length of the lens and is usually expressed in inches or millimeters. This focal length, in turn, is the measure of the size of an image that will be formed on the film when the lens is at a certain distance from the object.

It can be demonstrated that, whereas the image of an object six feet high and 25 feet from a lens would appear on the film or ground glass of a camera as ¼th inches high when the lens is of a one inch focal length, the image would be *twice* as tall if we used a two inch focal length lens and *ten* times as tall if a ten inch lens were used. This is the simplest way of describing the difference in the appearance of the height of a building as photographed from the same point with lenses of varying focal lengths.

A small camera is useful for "report" pictures like this one. Here a 2¼ x 2¼ Hasselblad was used. Islandia Hotel-Restaurant, San Diego, California. Frederick Liebhardt & Eugene Weston III; Vince Bonini, Architects.

The area shown on the ground glass around the figure or object is determined by the covering quality, or power, of the lens. All lenses of a given focal length, regardless of their design, will produce the same size of image on a film when the camera is at a fixed distance from the object. Because of the variance in covering power, however, lenses of the same focal lengths will produce a larger or smaller area around the image that is being photographed. In other words, if we are photographing a person in front of a building, a lens made to cover a wide field will show more of the building behind him because it takes in wide angles of light rays. A lens of the same focal length made to cover a narrower field will produce the same size of image of the person but will show less of the building.

It is this difference in the covering power that makes it possible to move in closer to a building with a wide angle lens than with a lens of narrower covering power of the same focal length. We have learned that the angle of view of a lens is independent of the focal length. A good example of this is evident in the Biogon lens produced by Carl Zeiss. This lens will cover a full 90° angle of field and is most satisfactory for architectural photography. The lens is manufactured in various focal lengths according to the same optical formula. It can be obtained in a 21mm size for 35mm cameras, 38mm size to be used on the 2¼ x 2¼ Hasselblad Superwide camera, or 75mm for 4 x 5 cameras. In every instance the covering power is the same but the focal length is proportionately longer so as to adequately cover the size of film in each camera.

If we measure the diagonal of the film in a 4 x 5 camera we will find that it is 6⅜ inches. A lens with this (6⅜ inches) focal length is said to be normal for a 4 x 5 camera. This means that the proportions of images are realistic and as seen by the eye. For certain types of record and documentary photography this is desirable. However it is more often advantageous to use a lens of somewhat wider angle (or covering power) than normal. This is particularly so when one needs to move in closer to a scene and still get a relatively complete view of the area. News photographs often fall into this category as do architectural details. Since the image will cover more film area at closer range, it can be reduced by changing the focal length; the next focal length lens desirable would be one approximately 5 inches.

No matter at what aperture a lens may be set, it has only one point of critical sharpness at each setting. In other

Three feet to 18 miles! The photographer need not be restricted by depth of field problems as can be seen in the picture. Cross-lighting of the interiors has accentuated textures and materials. This was taken at dusk with floodlights. Residence, Palm Springs, California. Thornton Ladd, Architect.

words, when focused at a specific distance, objects in front of and behind the plane will not be as sharp as the actual point of focus. The term "depth of field" of a lens, therefore, refers to the distance between the closest and farthest points, in front of and behind the point of critical focus that will be of an acceptable sharpness or definition. Depth of field varies because not all lenses are ground to the same optical formula. For architectural work a lens characterized as having great depth of field would be desirable.

When a lens is "stopped" down to a smaller aperture we refer to a change in the ratio between the focal length of the lens and the diameter of the lens. An 8″ focal length lens which measures ½″ in diameter is said to be an f/16 lens just as an 8″ focal length lens with a diameter of 1″ would be an f/8 lens. There is a mathematical ratio between the diameter of a lens and the amount of light transmitted. Doubling an aperture from ½″ to 1″, for example, allows *four* times the amount of light to enter the lens.

The change in shutter speed, therefore, would only be ¼th the previously required speed. This explains why exposure time is increased or decreased every time a lens opening is changed. When a lens is focused the aperture must be closed until all objects within a desired range of depth are brought into relative sharpness. The smaller the lens opening, the greater this range will be and as previously explained, the longer the exposure. The properties of each lens should be understood so that each exposure will be based on obtaining the maximum required exposure with adequate sharpness and tonal range.

The wider angle lens creates new effects in the photograph. Perspective is increased causing walls or other elements of a structure to appear longer and higher than normal. This effect is not always undesirable, but the wider the angle covered by the lens, the more pronounced it becomes and the photographer must use his judgment as to the limits to be set on this phenomenon.

As the width increases, the farthermost areas in a scene are correspondingly diminished. This effect is illustrated in some of the photographs that follow.

The introduction of more floor and ceiling space, plus an additional wall area, or even two, into a scene, is what gives the viewer the dimensional quality so significant in an architectural composition. However, there are certain occasions when a wide angle lens is unnecessary: when only a detail is required, for instance, or when working with color film since

27

With the camera set in completely neutral position the result is a disturbing falling away of perspective and an uninviting foreground.

The building restored. The camera was adjusted so that perspective lines were organized to avoid excessive foreground. Long Beach Water Department, Administration Building, Long Beach, California. Heusel, Homolka Associates, Architects.

In photographing a building, it is necessary to explore all areas for orientation and time of day. Ideally two sides of the building should be shown for dimensional quality. Below, the photograph has been taken from across a highway and uses existing landscaping as foreground. A wide angle lens has been used.

Here the same building has been photographed at a considerable distance since access onto the site was difficult; it was necessary to use an 8" lens in order to bring the building fairly close to the camera. This photograph, although clearly defining the structure, loses the dimensional and height quality of the one opposite. Actually it appears in the same scale as would an architectural model. Signal Oil and Gas Company Building, Los Angeles, California. Charles Luckman Associates, Architects (successors to Pereira & Luckman).

This was a wall-to-wall tile job in a school. Unfortunately an improper lens (the Schneider Angulon) was used and cut-off (black shadow at bottom) was caused by its lack of covering power. A lens such as the Super Angulon 90mm, instead of a regular wide angle lens, would have provided a clear image to the very bottom of the photograph. Also, if the girls had been placed so that their long skirts were hidden by the stair rail the photograph would not have become so dated. The camera was pointed down at a sharp angle to show the stairway; the front and back were then tilted to restore the vertical lines. Several extension flash lights were used to balance the strong outdoor and penetrating sunlight. Rosemead High School, Rosemead, California.

this produces a dimensional quality of its own by separation of tones and planes.

One of the most important things about a lens is its ability to cover a given negative size. This refers to the lens' optical ability to admit the desired image in equal light intensity to all areas of the negative. Often, when using various movements on a view camera, the resultant position of the lens in relation to the film is a far from normal one. Without proper optical quality, the lens is not able to transmit correctly and parts of the negative are exposed unequally. This results in black curved areas on the photographs. This may not be too serious if portions of a ceiling or sky can be cropped off in enlarging but much of the composition is usually destroyed.

Some lenses have perfected covering power and it is imperative that they be used. For wide angle work, a 90mm lens for a 4 x 5 camera is highly satisfactory. At this writing the most commonly used wide angle lens for architectural work requiring extreme camera movements has been the Schneider Super Angulon. It has an almost uncanny covering power and when used with a camera such as the Sinar, extreme corrections can be made with no cut-off. The Sinar has a unique bag-type bellows giving greater flexibility.

When photographing a scene not requiring a wide angle lens it is possible to obtain a narrower angle (longer focal length) lens of high covering power. That is, there is a substantial difference between a Kodak Ektar lens and a Dagor lens of the same focal length. This means that for architectural subjects requiring camera movements for adjustment of distortion the Dagor will produce the same general quality of negative as the Super Angulon mentioned above. In other words, the Ektar lens was essentially designed for other purposes than architectural photography. The Ektar lens is rated at f/4.7, and is a faster lens which makes it suitable for action or news photography for which it was actually designed. The Dagor is only f/6.8, and being slower because of the type of optical design, is more corrected for covering power. The photographer, obviously, must obtain the best advice and study each lens he intends to purchase for its maximum covering power.

For certain purposes a third category of lenses must be considered, those of focal lengths longer than usual. For 4 x 5 camera this would be any focal length above approximately 6⅜ inches. For architectural details, a so-called narrow lens is desirable. Apart from this, it is not advisable to use lenses of long focal lengths except for special purposes such as obtaining a view of a building not accessible from a place close enough for a normal or wide angle lens. A narrow lens, especially one of twice normal focal length, has the effect of compressing a subject.

The careful selection and use of proper lenses is extremely important. The photographer must never stop experimenting with his equipment.

The Film

Film, according to the technical announcements of manufacturers, has such qualities that the photographer can almost attain the millenium without bothering with a camera—the film exposes itself. This is far from true and only experience can dictate the best film for the particular job at hand. Almost every brand and type of film has its own qualities and properties but the photographer will find his needs can be satisfied without too much difficulty.

The degree of contrast in the range of tones registered varies with the type of film. Kodak Super-XX Panchromatic, for example, a medium speed film, has a softer contrast characteristic than most faster film. A film of this type is, therefore, desirable for scenes of extreme contrast range. It is possible to expose for deep shadow detail yet retain sufficient quality in the more brilliant areas to produce a print of excellent tonal values. Not all negatives possess the same contrast range with normal development. Higher speed film must compromise some of its range for speed.

Experimental exposures should be taken under a wide variety (including extremes) of conditions so as to compare the contrast and range of various brands of negatives. It is thus possible to understand negative response to many variations of light. Architectural subjects with deep overhangs, shaded patios and terraces, or with materials of varied surface, require skillful exposure techniques.

Medium, and even high speed, low grain emulsion film is available from any of the manufacturers. Tests with high contrast and flat-lighted subjects will quickly determine what film performs best under each situation. A full and fair period of use should follow each test. The finished prints and negatives should be analyzed objectively by experts, including printers and engravers, to fully weigh reproduction quality. Enlargements of small sections of negatives should be studied for graininess.

The range of film speed for black and white and color film is so wide that it can be confusing. Fortunately the manu-

This view was taken with a 12" lens on a 4 x 5 camera from a high vantage point (the closest possible) to illustrate the picturesque setting of this seaside sanctuary. Note the relationship of the steeple to the horizon Wayfarers' Chapel, Palos Verdes, California. Lloyd Wright, Architect.

A Roman Villa, modern style, taken with a wide angle lens. The disturbing diminution of the building and elongation of the pool and walkway seemed of doubtful value.

facturers include a clearly defined chart for exposures under varying conditions as well as complete data for developing each package of film.

However, there are individual circumstances needing clarification. There is a definite relationship among film speed, shutter speed, and lens aperture. By learning this it is possible to avoid many problems. Suppose that a building is being photographed with a 4 x 5 camera and the approach consists of a fountain and landscaped parkway 100 feet from the entrance to the building. If the architect wants to show the fountain in relationship to the entry it no doubt could be done with the use of a normal lens. This would reproduce, as discussed in the section on lenses, a realistic visual perspective. The fountain would appear in the photograph at the same apparent distance from the building as seen by the eye. In order to bring into focus both the fountain and the building it would be necessary to study the depth of field chart that usually accompanies each lens. It would reveal the distance at which the camera should be focused to provide sharpness in all areas. The fountain could be 20 feet from the camera thus requiring a depth of field from 20 to 100 feet. We may find by the chart, or by looking through the ground glass if a view camera is being used, that with the normal lens an aperture of f/32 and a shutter speed of 1/10ths seconds is required. This would take into consideration the filter factor of 2 for a yellow filter to darken the sky, desirable so as to produce a separation of the water of the fountain from the sky (see later discussion on filters). The above exposure would be the approximate one for a medium speed film. Now if the water movement was swift a shutter speed of 1/10th second would not be sufficient to stop the action.

What to do? The depth of field of the lens is fixed. So is the film speed. If a higher shutter speed, say 1/25th seconds, were used it would require a corresponding opening of the lens aperture to compensate for the more rapid exposure. The f/32 stop would not permit the entire field to be in focus. The answer is simple! Use a faster film which would make it possible to expose the scene at the required f/32 yet at the shutter speed of 1/50th second.

Another solution is possible although it would be a compromise in that it would involve the use of a wider angle lens. The wider the angle, the shorter the focal length and greater the depth of field. A 90mm lens would have such a depth of field that it would be possible to photograph the above scene at adequate speed even with medium speed film. However,

the compromise referred to would involve the size of the entry in proportion to the fountain. We have learned that the shorter the focal length lens for a given film size the smaller the image at a given distance as compared with a lens of longer focal length. It would be satisfactory to use the wide angle lens if the architect were willing to lose the apparent size of the entry. He would gain a longer appearing walkway because of the increased perspective of the lens. Slower color film in a 4 x 5 camera would introduce other depth of field problems. Higher speed professional color film is available but not yet in as high an ASA rating as black and white.

Because our problem here is twofold, speed to stop the action of the fountain and sufficient depth of focus for full sharpness, we can approach it from another tack. We can use a smaller film size camera. Suppose that we use a Hasselblad or Rolleiflex camera with a normal lens. Since a normal lens for a smaller film size has a greater depth of field we have here the best solution for our problem. The field covered by each camera, 2¼ x 2¼ and 4 x 5, would be the same since both would be using a normal focal length lens. But normal for 2¼ x 2¼ is substantially a shorter focal length, 3½ inches as opposed to 6⅜ inches, and the increased depth of field would do the job. Certainly for most purposes the sharpness of the negative would permit adequate enlarging even for exhibit size prints. Color transparencies would be sharp enough to reproduce with complete fullness of color and texture.

Furthermore, if one needed even a greater depth of field and/or faster shutter action, a 35mm camera could be used. Here again the relative images will be the same as for the larger cameras but with a still shorter focal length another increase of depth of field exists. With careful processing satisfactory 8 x 10 glossy prints can be made for reproduction and display from 35mm negatives. To further demonstrate the tremendous depth of field of a 50mm (normal) lens on a 35mm camera it is possible to focus at about 30 feet and achieve a depth of focus from 15 feet to infinity at an aperture of f/8.

The above hypothetical problem is indicative of what may confront the beginner. The fountain could just as well be a child in a playground in a scene taken for a story on a school for an architectural magazine in which the editor requested action. Flexible thinking and thorough understanding of theory and practice are indispensable.

A much neglected technique, the use of infra red film,

Without moving the 4 x 5 camera the 90mm wide angle lens was replaced with a 5″ lens. Now observe how much more clearly the elements of the house and adjacent areas appear. An extension flash was syncronized to prevent the interiors at the right from becoming a cave. Residence, Los Angeles, California. William L. Pereira Associates, Architects.

*Vivid delineation of background need not be
limited to exterior use of infrared film.
Here No. 50 flashbulbs were used to balance
outside brightness making it possible
to fully utilize the qualities of the film.
Pavilion, Lake Arrowhead, California.
David Fowler, Architect.*

offers many surprising and dramatic rewards to the inquisitive. An otherwise dull landscape scene or a hazy atmospheric background can spring into powerfully dynamic contrast with its use. Clouds barely seen by the eye or panchromatic film are vividly rendered, and foliage becomes a lacy white. Water in a pool or lake turns black, with clouds beautifully reflected. Under certain circumstances a summer landscape is transformed into a wintry scene.

The film must be used with a deep red filter. Although slow rated, the film can be exposed at f/22 and 1/5th or 1/10th seconds, an adequate depth of focus and shutter combination for most architectural landscapes. Development can be in the same developer and time as ordinary panchromatic film.

Color offers perhaps the most gratifying and certainly the most expressive medium in photography. Not only are the results visually satisfying but the expanded use of color in editorial and advertising media has offered photographers unlimited opportunities to explore and experiment. Manufacturers have kept pace in their development of various films. The most widely used for reproduction purposes is the reversal type, so named because in processing a positive transparency is produced. This type of film is best represented by Anscochrome, Kodak Ektachrome, and Kodachrome. In general the first two are quite similar in their properties. There are certain variations to their response to various colors and this must be investigated by the photographer. It is wise to use both films on the same assignment or experimental work and then compare them afterwards, color for color. Too much emphasis cannot be placed on the need for careful exposure and lighting. Once a sheet of color film has been exposed there is no manipulation possible in the darkroom as there is with black and white printing. Positive color transparencies are most often used for display or projection (35mm, 2¼ x 2¼). If the film does not fully express all the qualities of the original scene it is a failure because color film can reproduce every visible (and even invisible) nuance of the spectrum.

As well as for viewing and projection, a color transparency can be used for printing by photomechanical methods, dye transfer processing, or by printing on Type C material through color internegatives made from the transparencies. This last printing process offers more complete control of color tones and values than any other. It is best used when prints are made from color negatives.

Printing from color negatives is the most versatile, almost all-purpose color process developed to date. The color negative is developed from "negative-positive" film, the Kodak Ektacolor and Kodacolor films being the most prominent in this field. Because of certain technical phenomena inherent in these films they offer qualities for printing vastly superior to positive transparency material.

Other features of the color negative are equally useful to the photographer. Color transparencies (positives) can be produced in any desired size and quantity from such negatives. This process is of importance to the maker of 35mm slides. The use of 35mm color slides in schools of art and architecture has grown so tremendously that it is difficult for many of the schools to obtain sufficient material. Mechanical duplicates of original 35mm slides are at best unsatisfactory since they are not very faithful to the originals. For this reason some organizations specializing in quantity 35mm work take their originals on Ektacolor 4 x 5. The resulting duplicate 35mm slides are far superior to and certainly more consistent and accurate than other processes. Also, it is possible to make black and white prints from color negatives. This is done on Kodak Panalure paper. No doubt we can look for even greater improvements in color photography, processing, and reproduction. The color negative is probably the forerunner for, as has already been proven, its versatility and high quality fulfill extensive demands. It is therefore advisable to learn something of the principles of color photography.

Filters

We are all familiar with the typical amateur Sunday snapshot of a scene at the beach, mountains, or desert. This is too often a bleak landscape with hardly any of the tonal values of the original scene. What happened to the drama and excitement of wind tossed breakers on the beach and billowy cloud masses in the sky? The answer is simple. The photographer did not use a filter over his lens. On a black and white photograph all the tonal values of nature from white through the intermediate gray tones to black can be captured by the selection of the proper filter.

Filters are usually made from organic dyes and manufactured in gelatin sheets. The sheets are cut into various sizes and used over lenses to control the light coming through the lens. To protect its delicate surface the gelatin is almost always mounted between glass of high optical quality. The first part of this discussion will be on the use of filters in

Even black and white photographs can convey the lyrical beauty of spring and infrared film reproduces the delicacy and brightness of new foliage. With it red brick becomes lighter as does the green grass. The building is thus delineated with complete clarity. Stephens College Chapel, Columbia, Missouri. Eero Saarinen, Architect.

The optimum moment of twilight must be anticipated to produce balanced interior and exterior scenes. Daylight flash and film have been used in this case. Residence, Los Angeles, California. John Lautner, Architect.

black and white photography with emphasis on their use to obtain maximum pictorial effects and technical correctness.

The action of light through a filter is best understood if one studies the fundamental principles of light. Sunlight is made up of all the spectrum colors. This is why we see the colors of a rainbow when light passes through a prism; and the rainbow itself is caused by the light of the sun being broken up by passing through rain drops which act as prisms.

A filter is used to halt certain of the colors present in light and to allow others through the lines. This is the simplest definition of filter action and should be remembered.

The basic, or primary colors, are blue, green, and red. When combined they form white light as we see it in daylight. An object appears to be colored because it *reflects* that part of the spectrum and absorbs the other colors. In other words, a green filter appears green because it absorbs everything but green. The most commonly used filter is yellow. That is because yellow filters absorb blue and allow the red and green rays to pass and the latter combine to form yellow (as we might remember from our finger painting days). Therefore, since the primary reason for using a filter for outdoor scenes is to reduce the blue rays from the sky, the photographer generally uses what is called a K-2 filter; this is a medium yellow and does not affect the other colors to an appreciable degree. Since the blue is mostly absorbed, that part of the negative does not receive the amount of light it would have without the filter. Therefore it is in effect underexposed. On making a print we find that the sky prints dark and if clouds are present their white masses will stand out in clear definition. Hence no more Sunday snapshot blank skies.

Varying degrees of sky tones can be obtained according to the filter used. A medium red filter will darken the sky much more than the K-2 and a dark red filter will produce an almost black sky. The photographer must use his own judgment about the effect desired. At this point it is perhaps wise to point out that the effect of a filter depends upon the exposure. That is why some beginners are puzzled when they do not get the expected darkened skies. A filter will produce its optical effect best when the exposure for the scene is normal or even slightly under. This is not difficult when the light on the primary object is bright or at least equal to the light from the sky. But it is not always possible particularly when the scene in the composition may be a building, terrace, or patio which is partly or mostly in the shade or in the case of a building which has broad overhangs or deep reveals. The

The upper photograph has been taken without a filter, the lower one with. The orange filter used required an exposure about three times that of the upper picture. The exposure was specifically for sky values; longer exposure would have gained more detail in dark areas but would have "burned" out the sky. Residence, Hollywood Hills, California. Raphael S. Soriano, Architect.

additionally required exposure to get the subject will over-expose the sky and the filter will have little or no effect, producing a blanked out sky. This can only be counteracted by darkroom manipulation (see p. 71) where the sky is darkened by additional exposure from the enlarger.

When dark green masses of foliage are to be lightened a green filter will hold back the other color allowing the green to pass and register more strongly on the negative. For red or orange tones in need of better separation against building, landscapes or sky a red filter should be used.

In photographing architecture, however, care must be exercised not to overdo the use of filters. For example, if a building is set among trees and has a dark painted overhang or deep toned roofing materials a yellow or red filter would most likely produce a bad effect. The sky would go dark and this would approximate the tone of the roof and foliage; separation would be lost. It is wiser to use a green filter on this situation for this lightens the foliage without affecting the sky as much as would a yellow or red filter.

In the photography of brick structures, particularly dark red brick, a dark yellow or a red filter lightens the tone so that the brick stands out against the sky or surrounding darker objects.

Obviously, these suggestions should not be strictly adhered to; every photographer should experiment with as many variations of exposure and filters as possible and by a careful analysis of the results establish a working pattern. It must be pointed out that with each change of filter a change of exposure is required. This is because each filter has a factor, usually given in the form of a number; the factor refers to the time of exposure required to compensate for the amount of light absorbed by the filter. The most commonly used yellow filter has a factor of 2. This simply means that the exposure required is two times normal. If the normal exposure would have been 1/100 seconds, the filter compensation would require 1/50 seconds. Or, if a speed shot is necessary to capture action or stop the movement of leaves against a sky, the opening of the lens one stop would produce the same effect; from f/32 to f/22, as an example, which admits twice the amount of light at a given speed.

Once the photographer has familiarized himself with the basic uses of filters he can explore their special uses. One often sees effective moonlight scenes in motion pictures actually taken in broad daylight. These effects can be duplicated in still work by the use of deep red filters, in combination with light polarizing filters.

The polarizing filter is essential when photographing glass in architecture when reflections are bothersome. Since the filter is most effective when the camera angle is almost 35° from the plane of the subject, compositions are somewhat limited. For the reduction of glare from water or metallic objects the polarizing filter is indispensable. It is particularly useful in photographing buildings with porcelain enamel, tile, or aluminum surfaces.

The following suggestions are for the use of filters in interior photography. Basically, the desired effect must first be determined. If an interior contains an abundance of dark wood it may be best rendered by using a filter equivalent to the tone of the wood. Redwood which is dark stained is rendered lighter by a red filter. Likewise yellowish wood requires a medium or deep yellow filter and is better reproduced if photographed with an orthochromatic film instead of panchromatic.

The simplest rule to remember for general purposes is as follows: A filter of the same color as the subject will pass the light from that subject. Since less, in proportion, of the other colors will reach the film the subject will appear lighter on the print.

In color work it is often necessary to compensate for balance of light, particularly on interior work. For example, in fluorescent lit areas it is necessary to change the Kelvin rating to the 3200° color temperature required for the type of film generally used for interior photographs in color taken with only artificial lighting. The Kelvin rating of fluorescent lighting is about 3500°. An 81B filter will reduce the temperature of the light to proper balance. Since color photography requires a considerable degree of experience it is advised that the data sheet accompanying each box of color film be carefully read. This will provide the most reliable data for the film in that particular box for there are often variations in the film from batch to batch. Every manufacturer provides complete and rapid service for their color and their field men are available all over the country to answer questions and offer suggestions on how to go about solving particular problems.

Finally, obtain from your dealer copies of various books on the subject of filters. The above information is intended to introduce the fundamental uses of filters but the subject is very important and further information should be sought.

Light Meters

An exposure meter is an instrument used to determine the light intensities of a given scene so that the lens aperture and shutter of the camera can be set to provide for an accurate exposure. There are two basic types of photoelectric cell meters: that which measures light reflected from the subject; that which measures incident light in a scene. Incident light is the over-all light from a scene as it reaches the camera. Whereas a reflected light meter is pointed at the subject to get direct reflection readings, the incident light meter is pointed toward the camera.

There are specific needs for the use of light meters when working on color interior assignments. Here a color meter as well as a light meter ought to be employed. The balancing of various light sources with widely varying Kelvin temperatures is impossible without one. However this type of assignment is not a common one and photographers can only learn from experience in this kind of work.

Pointing the meter at the widely varying intensities of the average exterior view of a building can be confusing. Perhaps as many as five, and more, widely differing readings are likely to be read from the meter in various directions. The decision on what exposure to use can only be obtained by tests. One must become acquainted with the meter, the film, and the developer to such an extent that before long it is possible to select the exact area at which to point the meter. The optimum exposure of the film for the particular range of tones desired to best express the building will soon be achieved.

There has been considerable progress in the design of exposure meters. The old workhorses, the Weston (No. 4) and the General Electric Golden Crown are as dependable as ever and have been improved to make them more sensitive and versatile. Both are medium priced meters. Another excellent meter, the Lunasix, is perhaps the most sensitive meter on the market. It has a range which will give an exposure meter reading of eight hours, if necessary and could almost give a reading in a dark room! On the other hand, it is so sensitive in greater light intensities that it can produce a reading for minute fractions of a second for extremely high speed photography. It reads light from about a 30-degree field, so it reads a relatively narrow field. This meter is quite expensive. In the lower priced field, the Gossen meter is small, efficient and inexpensively priced.

The most advanced photographic light meter is the Honeywell Pentax. This particular model, No. 321, is an expensive one but it is so perfect in its narrowness of field that it is possible to aim the meter at a scene at great distances and select, in the viewer of the finder, any one narrow spot from which one may wish to get a reading for specific exposure. If an intensely illuminated area is immediately adjacent to a dark shadowed area, it is possible to select at great distances the specific reading for each light value. This is the first meter of its kind that has been so successfully developed and no other meter on the market comes near it in such photographic light determination. The investment in so expensive a meter—one that covers a three-degree field of light—is worthwhile. Actually it solves most of the complaints made about other meters for it eliminates the great range of light values picked up by the wider angle light meter. It avoids the necessity, prevalent with wider angle meters, of having to walk in close to a scene to avoid the brighter elements in order to capture the more shadowed segments of a composition. In other words, this is the closest thing to instant light reading that has ever been achieved.

All of the meters so far mentioned are for measurement of reflected light. The Brockway meter measures incident light and is actually the old Norwood meter which was first introduced during the post-war years. The Brockway meter is ideal for balancing light conditions for it is used by walking into a scene and pointing the dome of the meter back towards the camera. The light setting for the interior illumination then can be adjusted until the exact reading is ascertained to within a few footcandles. This is a must for scenes, particularly in color, where the balance is critical. The Brockway meter is reasonably priced.

The foregoing are a representative group of meters with a wide price range. Price, however, is not indicative of efficiency in meter selection. The function of a meter is the determination of light and this can be obtained with almost any type of meter on the market to a relatively satisfactory degree. It is up to the photographer to study all the meters he can and then determine which will best serve his own needs.

It is possible, with experience and study, to forego the use of light meters for all but exceptional occasions. The best way for a beginner to go about this is to study the meter without using the camera at all. He should spend some time judging the exposure by eye and then checking against the meter to see how correct his reading was. In such a way he will begin to *feel* light and to understand its qualities and relative values. Regardless of much propaganda to the contrary, light intensity does not differ very radically from country to country. The discerning eye can soon learn to analyze the differences accurately without a meter.

Care should be taken in the use of the meter anyway. It

should not become a crutch. Metering a scene is arbitrary at best and the measurements must still be interpreted according to the photographer's desires.

Viewers and Projectors

Viewers and projectors for looking at slides are of great importance to the user of the 35mm camera. Some photographers and, particularly some schools, prefer to collect 2¼" x 2¼" slides. Viewers and projectors are available for this size, too, but the same things apply to this equipment as to that for 35mm slides. Projectors are necessary for judging quality in the studio; for demonstration of designs by designers to clients; for demonstration of photographic work by photographers to clients; and for lecture and classroom use in design schools, seminars, etc.

There are many types of viewers and projectors on the market. The simplest of the viewers is the hand one; the slides are placed into it individually and the viewer is held up to a light source (a window, light fixture, etc.). This kind of viewing is perfectly satisfactory so far as quality is concerned but is rather inconvenient in handling and for comparative estimates of slides.

Better types of viewers for these purposes are those operated by batteries or on 110-volt lines which provide a light source for viewing and are thus more consistent for estimating purposes.

Other viewers available are those that magnify the slides several times so that they can be viewed more easily and by more than one person at a time. Desk viewers are also quite good: the slides are dropped in from the top and a lever pressed for dropping them out at the bottom when viewing is finished; thus a quick sequence viewing is possible.

There are so many competent brands of viewers on the market that it would be unreasonable to recommend any specific ones. They should be tried out in the store before purchase.

Slide projectors are available in many brands and with various features. The most advanced of these is the remote control slide changer which can advance or reverse the sequence of change and operate focusing. This is, of course, the most expensive type; many perfectly adequate less complex mechanisms are available at lower prices. The naming of brands is unnecessary because there is scarcely an unsatisfactory one on the market. Select a screen for projection according to the size of image desired; there are many excellent ones on the market.

Lighting Equipment

It is so difficult to separate lighting equipment from on-site procedures that this whole subject is discussed under techniques in Chapter IV.

The Polaroid Adapter

It is possible to take Polaroid photographs with a 4 x 5 view camera. A Polaroid adapter which fits cameras with the standard graphic type back is available which makes it possible to get black and white prints on the spot in ten seconds. The new Polaroid film now has a negative element which is of high quality. This allows the making of enlargements on returning to the darkroom; an ideal arrangement for practicing in the field and for one use only assignments.

The Tripod

A good tripod is of great importance. It must be light yet sturdy. Its movements must literally have fingertip control. There should be quick and safe controls for height and adjustment to permit swift changes from worm's eye to giraffe's eye angles. The tripod must also have separate controls for tilting and swinging, permitting smooth movement and security with accuracy.

This may seem a difficult prescription to fill. Fortunately, several brands of tripod on the market have all these qualities. Test your own camera on several types. Does the camera mount easily without fiddling with undersized center screw control? Do the legs stay up when they are extended, or does the weight of the camera cause them to collapse? A slight turn of the leg extension controls should be sufficient to permit safe operation.

Since there are scores of brands of tripod on the market a carefully conducted search should be made for a suitable one. One of the most versatile of all tripods is the Tiltall Professional, #4602. This is a lightweight aluminum tripod with complete control facilities for ease in operation. It has a two-position head, making it possible to tilt the camera flexibly in any direction, control on the tripod for raising and lowering the center shaft, and locking devices for pivoting or panning. The legs can be extended so that the tripod will rise to something over seven feet in height. This tripod

For assignments requiring lightweight equipment these items fill the bill. The case contains all lights and accessories and the tripod and 2¼ x 2¼ Hasselblad camera are easily transportable.

is perhaps the best on the market for architectural photography for it will carry even the heavy 8 x 10 camera. It is manufactured by the Marchioni Company in Rutherford, N.J.

Another tripod of substantial quality and flexibility is the Safe-Lock made by Safe-Lock Company, Inc., Hialeah, Florida. Of the several models they make two are of particular interest for architectural photography. One is the Safe-Lock Speed made especially for the Graflex Company. It is a universal tripod with good leg extension but while it can be tilted in both directions, this latter feature is not as flexible as it could be. The other, less expensive model, the Flip-Lock, is actually the better of the two for our purposes. It, too, has good leg extension with a good locking control (the flip lock from which it derives its name) near the top of the tripod which saves bending for leg extension while the camera is on the tripod.

The Quickset Tripod is still one of the best and dependable standbys amongst the all-purpose tripods. Unfortunately, as is the difficulty with so many commercial tripods, it does not have control for tilting in both directions. Most tripods have just one control made primarily for the type of panning that one would use in motion picture work. Apparently manufacturers do not realize that photographers using still cameras must have more than just the panning head. It is for this reason that the Tiltall previously described, is so vastly superior to most other commercial tripods.

Linhoff makes an extremely flexible set of high quality tripods; amongst these one is almost sure to find one to fit most of his utilitarian needs.

There are scores of other brands but only a few have flexible enough heads to make them worth recommending. The old commercial wooden tripod can still be found and in fact, is still used by many old-time commercial organizations. However, it is heavy, bulky, and inflexible. It is preferred only on personal grounds.

Various heads are available which can be attached to some tripods and this is probably how the old type wood tripod can be used. But the lightweight metal ones, some of which are listed above, offer the best bet for the photographer who does not want to be handicapped by the mechanical problems of camera support.

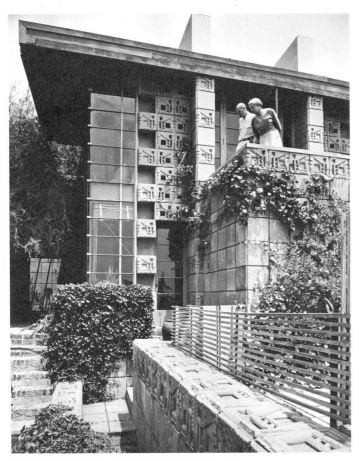

Freeman Residence, Hollywood, California. Frank Lloyd Wright, Architect.

The exterior of this house is shown on page 71—one occasion where photographic explanation was necessary. The dome revolves on a track to open this sitting area to the sky. Low intensity flash was synchronized to subdue blackness of shadows. Dome House, Cave Creek, Arizona. Soleri & Mills, Architects.

Film Processing

No professional photographer needs to be told how important the development, printing, and enlargement of his work is, but we are attempting to point out to the architect or other designer the importance not only of understanding how a professional gets good pictures but to be able to handle a camera himself with a modicum of skill. This is all very well but so often the amateur does not really ever see his photographic work at its best because he does not realize how very important the processing of his film actually is and he drops his precious films off at the drug store. If a picture is worth the film to take it on it is worth seeking out a competent laboratory to process it; these exist in all major cities. Like a good many things in life, finding the right laboratory may be something of a problem but the search is worthwhile. By having film processed in a good laboratory careful handling is insured. Negatives are handled with respect in the laboratory and prints can be made to order. The laboratory can often give hints on how to improve negatives and can be valuable in many other ways as well.

The Darkroom

The degree of quality and accuracy required in processing an architectural photograph necessitates an efficient darkroom routine. Everything in the darkroom must be kept at the highest degree of cleanliness. Negatives should be processed with a rigid adherence to time and temperature routing. Every film exposed must be a good one and the habit of taking "one more" shot should be eliminated from the photographer's practice.

There are a few conveniences which can be introduced into the darkroom which will help in making the work go more smoothly. For example, there are excellent timing devices for controlling exposures. To these can be coupled light intensity control units which aid in maintaining uniform light for negatives of varying densities when enlarging.

Another simple eye-saver is the wiring of the enlarger so that when it is turned on, the area's safelights automatically go off. This eliminates the excess light on the easel and permits clearer viewing of the image for judging exposure, focusing, and manipulation by dodging and flashing. As for developers, with scores of brands on the market it would be foolish to try to recommend even one. Which brand of shampoo do you use?

As has been previously stated the architecture must take precedence over the photograph. For the designer taking a photograph of his own this is an unnecessary warning but the amateur or professional photographer must always keep it in mind : the purpose of an architectural photograph may be documentary or interpretive, or both, but it is seldom the pure art of photography itself. It may, in the best examples, reach this level, but only when it first fulfills its purpose as an architectural photograph.

Even if the purpose of a photograph is purely documentary, however, the good photographer will use his imagination. The composition of the architectural photograph is extremely important. The photographer must be sufficiently aware of design to recognize its elements accurately and of photography to be able to compose an interpretive photograph. A façade or elevation of a building may be shown in any number of ways but it must be clearly understandable to the viewer of the photograph. Furthermore, photograph and structure must be related each to the other. It is all too easy to create photographic compositions which are misleading and well-nigh impossible, for the layman especially, to interpret (or even, on occasion, to recognize) rather than to produce photographic compositions which can be read with the plans of the building.

The camera often gets into positions not normally used by —or sometimes even possible to—human beings. The resultant photographs are often a shock to the designer himself. Another surprise lies in the use of the wide angle lens ; the perspective effects are often startling. A complaint occasionally heard about architectural photography is that it glamorizes the building ; this need not be true. Sometimes the complaint stems from such effects as we have just mentioned, sometimes because the camera has displayed a more discerning and critical eye than the human complainer.

The photographer's ultimate aim is to achieve, so far as it is possible in reproducing a three-dimensional form in two-dimensional terms, the full qualities of a design. However much editing a photographer may be obliged to do, he must keep this fact well in mind.

The section on lenses (Chapter III, page 23) describes the wonderfully flexible choice of glass with which the photographer may perform his work and the photography of a building can be achieved from practically any point of view. But it should be remembered that deliberately forshortened perspectives and the use of extreme wide angle lenses can

The measure of integration of a building with its surroundings can be shown by borrowing from a neighbor's area. Arts & Architecture Magazine Case Study House, La Jolla, California. Killingsworth, Brady & Smith, Architects.

*In this seldom-seen view of one of New York's
prominent buildings dramatization of simple
design elements has resulted in an eye-
stopping interpretation. Seagram Building,
New York, N.Y. Mies van der Rohe and
Philip Johnson, Architects.*

produce undesirable misrepresentations. Think twice before
shooting this kind of picture!

The study of as varied a selection of design publications
as possible is advisable for the budding professional (and,
indeed, amateur) photographer. Camera angles should be
analyzed for understanding design criteria as well as the
photographer's motives. The comments in Chapter I on the
development of the designer's and photographer's awareness should be carefully read. Perhaps awareness can be
considered the key to successful photography.

Two main areas of technical knowledge are involved in
photographic composition: one is camera angles, the other is
lighting, and we will tackle them in that order.

How much of a building should be shown in a composition?
What should determine the beginning and end of a composition? What lens should be used for the desired perspective,
field coverage, and rendering of proportion? How does the
structure relate to its site and neighboring buildings? The
elements of environment are certainly influential in the
design and should, therefore, be considered in the photographic presentation of the building.

The appearance of a building is effected by camera height.
Study of the composition on the ground glass with the camera at eye level and then at a foot or so above grade presents
a sharp lesson in scale. The low camera angle has the advantage of eliminating a messy skyline—telephone poles and
wires, vents, and other ugly superstructures. Or the building
on the block behind the building being photographed may
rear high into the sky. All of these situations can usually be
cured by the low camera position.

In some instances even the low position is not sufficient to
clean up a background. Retouching and airbrushing in the
studio is one way of dealing with it but it is more desirable
to change the camera angle since the scene can thus remain
a composed whole. A foreshortened perspective down the
facade can present a natural pedestrian point of view. A
wide angle lens is necessary for this type of view and the
result is almost always dramatic yet realistic. Details not
sufficiently pronounced in the long view picture can be photographed separately, perhaps with a normal lens.

It has been noted in Chapter III (page 27) that the view
camera has many controls essential for architectural photography which assist in manipulation and adjustment for perspective and proportion.

When a subject is to be photographed from a position
other than head-on (the one-point elevation position) there

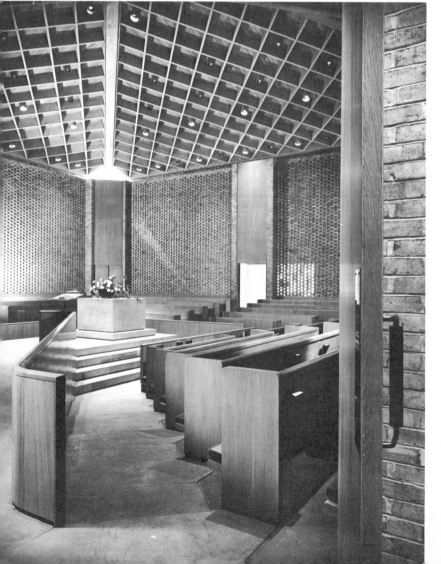

*Intricate design calls for a clear analysis of the
architect's concept and more than one view may be
necessary for understanding of the form and
purpose of the structure. Stephens College Chapel,
Columbia, Missouri. Eero Saarinen, Architect.*

The industrial form of the spiral staircase made an intriguing study in this "traditional" interior; it offered numerous possibilities for camera and lighting composition. In this scene it has served to frame the living room. Residence, Beverly Hills, California. William Sutherland Beckett, Architect.

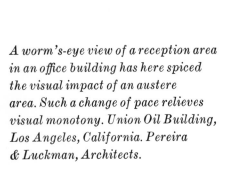

A worm's-eye view of a reception area in an office building has here spiced the visual impact of an austere area. Such a change of pace relieves visual monotony. Union Oil Building, Los Angeles, California. Pereira & Luckman, Architects.

50

will be a greater convergence of horizontal lines than is usually desired. To adjust them to realistic perspective, the camera back can be swung on its vertical axis until it is parallel to the front of the subject.

In other words, the plane of the film (the camera back) should be the same as that of the subject in all cases where distortion is to be minimized.

Camera angles depend on the type of lens to be used. The wide angle lens imposes a completely different discipline on the photographer than does the normal or narrow angle lens.

Inasmuch as wide angle lenses tend to introduce a quality of spaciousness and extended perspective, it is necessary to use them judiciously. It is possible to restore a more natural perspective to the length of a building, for instance, by using the horizontal swing of the view camera as described above. It is often necessary to move to one side of a subject because of limited space and it is in such situations that the horizontal swing of the camera proves extremely useful, restoring as it does the parallel lines that could otherwise only be got from a one-point elevation view. Even where a one-point elevation would be physically possible, it is often more desirable to move to one side to avoid the flatness of a sheer façade picture (particularly if taken with a normal angle lens) or to give more information about the design as a whole than is possible with a head-on picture. In the pictures of the church on page 54, for instance, it was necessary to show how the roof appeared on a side view in relation to the front. To the left was an obstruction which made it necessary to set up the camera in a position closer to the building than was desirable with the normal angle lens then on the camera. To solve the problem, the lens was replaced with a wide angle one; the back of the camera was swung so as to keep the lines of the building as parallel as possible in the picture. This retained the simple, yet strong, architectural feeling of the building and the side view of the steeple gave a three-dimensional delineation in the picture.

The picture of the swimmers (page 55) was a problem of depth of focus, fast film, and horizontal perspective. It would have been possible to swing the camera back to a greater degree but this would diminish the apparent length of the structure in the background; this was avoided and the effect is still natural. The movements of the camera front and back were adjusted so that it was possible to stop the action of the racing dives of the swimmers. Without these adjustments the camera position would have been uncorrected, the exposure f/32 at 1/50th seconds, and the film a fast one. With

Outdoor living as exemplified by the interrelationship of garden terrace and indoor room space should be photographed with as natural a setting as possible. Residence, West Los Angeles, California. Cliff May, Designer. Courtesy House & Garden, Condé Nast Publications.

The house was a new one and had not been landscaped. However the architect needed a photograph immediately. The lower picture shows the result of borrowing the neighbor's bushes. Simply dropping the tripod legs brought into prominence a pleasing landscape mass which almost literally gives the new house a garden setting. This, indeed, is just how the house appears to the neighbors across the street when they view it from their garage entrance. Residence, California. Dale Naegle Associates, Architects.

A slight fraction of a side of a building adds dimension and perspective to a photograph. But such a view can create a disturbing angle to the front of the building. Hard to believe but, like a giraffe's neck, the correctly operated view camera can stretch and adjust its point of view. In the lower picture the receding left end of the building has been restored to an almost natural visual perspective. Northrop Corporation, Nortonics Division Building, Palos Verdes, California. Charles Luckman Associates, Architects.

*The upper picture is sharp and formal but leaves the viewer with a need for more information.
The addition of dimension in the lower picture supplies it but without camera correction the front
of the building would have faded away off the picture. Notice that the rectangular form has
been retained and that the design of the roof elements has become understandable. Church of the
Resurrection, Cedar Rapids, Iowa. Crites & McConnell, Architects.*

the adjustments the exposure was f/11 at 1/250th seconds. To bring the foreground into sharp focus with the rest of the scene, the lens was tilted forward on its horizontal axis.

We have discussed the variations in camera placement and/or angles in exterior scenes. On interiors camera placement and adjustments are just as critical. Generally speaking, the interiors of contemporary buildings tend to be particularly closely related to the design of the structure as a whole. To convey this fact in a photograph it is very necessary to compose scenes relating the two elements. Camera angles dictate furniture placement, so the photographer must learn to relocate furniture specifically for his compositions. Although the actual appearance of this rearrangement often shocks the designer, who may arrive on the scene, the photographer's judgment must be accepted for the purposes of the photograph.

The study of interior photographs is essential for the inexperienced photographer if he wishes to produce good pictures of interior design. The photographer, if working without the assistance of the designer, must assume his rôle for his own purposes.

As a demonstration, try standing behind a chair or table in a room. Looking across the room, observe how much of the floor is visible. Now slowly lower your line of vision and note that the foreground furniture begins to cut into the floor. There may be a point where the floor becomes completely hidden. The photographer must decide how much of the floor is to be shown. Because camera height effects the appearance of an area so considerably, all aspects of the composition must be weighted.

A low camera position makes the room look higher and gives an illusion of a more expansive floor area. This view will make individual furniture pieces less important. It may in any case be necessary to move furniture aside where the shot is to be a long view towards a fireplace or other important feature as focal point. Where the floor covering is the focal point texture and expanse are the primary elements and the low angle shot gives the best results.

A high camera angle will show a free space relationship between furniture pieces and will place a greater emphasis on the floor area, as opposed to its textures. For textural emphasis of ceilings the high camera angle produces the best effects. The room or interior area will not appear to be as tall with the higher camera position as with the lower one.

Catching a fast getaway like this requires an increase of depth of focus by manipulation of camera and shutter speed. Recreation Center, Buena Park, California. Richard J. Neutra, Architect.

Here a composition which would show the complete integration of interior and architectural design was demanded. Residence, Beverly Hills, California. Rex Lotery, Architect.

It must be remembered that visual qualities of an area differ considerably from photographic ones, especially when a wide angle lens is used. With practice one can learn to "see" a wide angle perspective almost immediately so that the choice of lens width for full coverage becomes almost second nature. For study purposes pictures can be taken from various angles, at various camera heights with, if possible, a number of lenses. Polaroid exposures are a good idea, permitting as they do immediate examination of results.

A church interior is a good subject for such a study and we will describe a series of possible views and their results.

If the camera is placed in the nave at a normal eye level height and fitted with a wide angle lens, the nave will appear to be longer than normal in the resulting picture. Proportionately, the chancel will appear approximately half normal size. With the groundglass in a vertical position, the church will appear long and the height accentuated. The eye level height will create an uncomfortable down hill perspective along the rows of pews. This is caused by the rapidly diminishing perspective effect of a wide angle lens. To reduce this uncomfortable effect, the camera should be lowered to a height just over the top of the pews. This will produce a more appealing reading. The pews will appear higher and in better relationship to the height of the church. Also, the separation between the pews will have a more natural visual appearance.

The camera remained in a fixed position for all three of these pictures; lens changes produced the different effects. Although very bold, the wide angle view (above) has almost lost the chancel. The normal lens used in the picture to the left on this page is completely natural in its rendering of the proportion between masses. The narrow angle lens view (facing page) is necessary for illustration of significant and unusual design elements. First Methodist Church, Glendale, California. Flewelling, Moody & Horn, Architects.

Careful observation of sunlight and cloud shadows produced this vivid demonstration of an unusual architectural concept. A second camera had been set up for this view so as to be ready for a break in the clouds to the west. Work continued on the interior (see page 38) in the interim. Residence, Los Angeles, California. John Lautner, Architect.

The early bird. This was a north-facing house and early morning northeast sunlight had to be caught for effective illustration. Residence, West Los Angeles, California. Jones & Emmons, Architects.

However, even at that the chancel will still appear reduced in size. At this point a more normal (approximately 125mm on a 4 x 5 camera) focal length lens, replacing the wide angle, will produce a more natural rendering of the chancel's actual size in proportion to the length of the nave.

To analyze the difference between the wide and normal angle views is of vital importance. The demonstration will indicate that the only physical advantages of the wide angle lens are the extended perspective and height effects. On the other hand, the normal lens will create a favorable perspective on the long nave while presenting a considerably more normal dimension in the apparent size of the chancel.

Where a candid snapshot kind of scene is required the smaller hand camera with high speed film is most useful and can catch the actual workings of a building, plant, or street scene depicting the orientation of the building to the site. The results of this type of shot are more atmospheric than the slicker, polished photograph of the larger camera. The latter kind of photograph is more suitable where a carefully studied and composed picture depicting architectural elements is required.

Sometimes it is necessary to get both naturalness and accuracy of detail—in a school scene, for example. Special playground activities or classroom scenes can be taken with a small camera fitted with a wide angle lens so that the architectural elements of the area are well defined and yet the activities do not get too posed in appearance.

Lighting

Experience teaches that photographs can be taken under any lighting conditions, with or without sunlight, and even in the rain. It is important to realize this fact and to make use of it where necessary for a sudden deadline or a long period of inclement weather. Photography under these conditions should be tried quite often to gain familiarity with color and light values. Color values in so-called dull weather are often rich and true in tone and while it means sacrificing a postcard blue sky, the experience of absorption will prove invaluable and the results can be gratifying, as in the color version of the picture on page 64.

Buildings are not always situated on the proper side of the sun so architectural photographers must learn to make their own sun. It is possible to make up for lack of sunshine by effective perspective and artificial lighting of interiors. It is even possible to create a twilight effect by manipulation in the darkroom (see page 70).

It rained all day and the house faced east. Ideally morning sunlight should have been used for the view over the pool but the clouds did not dissipate until sunset and it was not possible to wait another day. As a solution the interior was illuminated with floodlights, a flash was placed over the camera, and the film was exposed for the deeper tonal values of the landscape. This method has reproduced the delicate shadow textures on the interiors and fields while the flash on the camera has illuminated the fascia of the house and the poolside rocks and garden. Since the sky was bright with late afternoon sunlight, darkroom dodging was used to restore tonal qualities. Residence, Ojai, California. Richard J. Neutra, Architect.

59

The imposing new architectural forms of today's structural technology are exciting to photograph. In this case the gleam of sunlight illuminated the building's major support column; another instance of the use of time of day for effective photography. Residence, Cedar Rapids, Iowa. Crites & McConnell, Architects.

Nevertheless, it is better to work whenever possible in the light and weather conditions which most nearly approximate the effects required in the photograph because the quality of a picture taken under bad conditions can only roughly simulate that obtainable under ideal conditions.

It is truly remarkable how many people do not know that in the Northern Hemisphere the sun rises in the northeast and sets in the northwest during summertime. This means that buildings with broad overhangs receive no sunshine on the south side for a period of several weeks in late spring and early summer; and that in early spring and late fall the situation is reversed and ideal lighting is attained on the south facade of a building at mid-morning and mid-afternoon. Buildings facing east or west offer best year-round control possibilities throughout the day.

A compass, incidentally, is a useful piece of pocket equipment. All too often no-one knows where north is except for such information as, "about that tree, I think." With a knowledge of the sun's position throughout the day and the building's orientation, an hour by hour course can be charted where necessary (which is usually on a complete structure assignment).

The exact position of the sun should be carefully noted on all exterior jobs for this is the secret of dramatic shadow effects. Some of them are short-lived and if the camera is not set in preparation the light is gone before the camera is ready. The author often works with two view cameras, keeping one set up in advance when working with rapidly changing sun-shadow compositions. On a cloudy day one cannot wait for a break so a camera should be left set up for a quick dash outside to get a vital scene. If a second view camera is not available, an adequate hand camera (such as the 2¼ x 2¼ Superwide Hasselblad or a 35mm camera fitted with a wide angle lens) will serve the purpose very well.

Also, notice how effectively natural light floods an interior at certain hours. Learn to use it, especially for color work. In many commercial buildings existing light is provided by continuous fluorescent lighting fixtures and often the ceilings in commercial and public buildings consist of continuous luminous panels. In such cases additional lighting by the photographer is almost completely unnecessary. The existing light is generally of such high foot-candle values that further artificial lighting is superfluous.

For most interior shots, however, natural or existing artificial lighting is either unsuitable or insufficient and anyone

wishing to take a truly effective interior picture will almost invariably have to provide supplementary lighting. He should, however, make himself familiar enough with the properties of common types of architectural lighting systems to be able to use them flexibly without having to carry endless varieties of equipment for every situation he could possibly encounter. Before setting up his lighting equipment the photographer should make sure that the building's wiring and outlets can carry the extra load which can be quite high if several flood and spotlights are used. It is wise to locate circuits in separate parts of a building by checking the circuit breakers or fuse boxes.

Lighting Equipment

Since most photography work is on location, lighting equipment should be readily portable, light in weight, and simple to maintain and operate. The main items of equipment which the architectural photographer will find necessary are floodlights, spotlights, a flashgun, a booster box, and adequate extension cords, flashbulbs, and reflectors.

Various sizes of reflectors are available in all camera supply stores. The small lightweight aluminum ones designed to use the smallest floodlight bulb and designated as #1 by manufacturers, are perfectly adequate for limited areas; they are about 10″ in diameter. However, a slightly larger reflector, made to utilize a #2 floodlamp and about 12″ to 14″ in diameter, will give a more intense and generally broader light. The large #4 size is used mainly for commercial work and is cumbersome.

Since numerous brands of reflectors are available it is not possible to make specific recommendations. The reflectors selected should have barndoors—metal hinged visors which are used to control the extent of light beam. Not all reflectors come equipped with barndoors so this should be checked.

Although it is desirable to use spotlights which have adjustable width beams they are usually too heavy and large to transport along with the volume of other lights and equipment. Simple mushroom type spot bulbs offer an efficient substitute. These bulbs, of the type used in store displays and outdoor lighting, are available in a wide range of wattages, and in narrow and medium spot beam and even in wide flood beams. They can be placed in regular reflectors or in sockets which come with clamps for attaching to light stands or any fixed object such as the edge of a shelf or door. A barndoor attachment which fits directly on the bulb is also available—a most handy device for controlling the spot beam.

Lightweight stands are available for all of the above-mentioned equipment. Since the photographic requirements for interior work often involve the use of flashbulbs for balancing daylight and interior lighting, reflectors suitable for this purpose should be chosen. Some reflectors have deep sockets to accept the long neck of the #2 floodlamp but the considerably shorter neck of the flashbulb will not fit these sockets. It is important that the reflector socket depth be carefully chosen.

Flashbulbs provide a light of high intensity and can be used in synchronization with the camera shutter permitting high speed action to be recorded yet balancing of interior with exterior daylight brilliance. For simple single light fill the bulb can be placed in a flashgun which is connected to the shutter by a cord. For the more complex lighting requirements of large or interrelated areas the use of a flashgun is not advisable and the firing of several bulbs in synchronization should be accomplished with a booster box.

This is a device which contains several outlets for connecting desired flash circuits, batteries for power, a pilot light wired as a test circuit to reveal when one of the lines may be defective because of a bad bulb or faulty circuit. In addition, the box has an outlet for an extension cord to reach the shutter for synchronized exposures. For some scenes where daylight balance is not critical it is possible to open the shutter with a cable release and press an auxiliary button on the booster box to fire the flash. A booster box is indispensable. It is absolutely foolproof with its indicating "test" circuit and capacity to produce enough power to fire almost any number of bulbs, even at synchronized shutter speeds. The box can be built by almost any camera repair establishment or photo technician. The savings on "unpopped" flashbulbs and time will soon pay for it.

Flashbulbs are wire or foil filled glass bulbs which when ignited by an electric current emit an instantaneous high intensity light. They can be used only once and are manufactured in a variety of sizes. These range from tiny fingertip ones to large #50 or #3 (depending on the manufacturer) sizes for intense light in large areas. The size of bulb selected will depend upon the area, its tones of walls, ceilings, or floor, and the quantity of daylight requiring balance. Since all of these are so very variable the beginner should start with a bulb of medium intensity such as a #11.

The rating of a bulb's output is listed according to a guide number. This is a constant and the table that is provided with each carton of bulbs demonstrates the calcu-

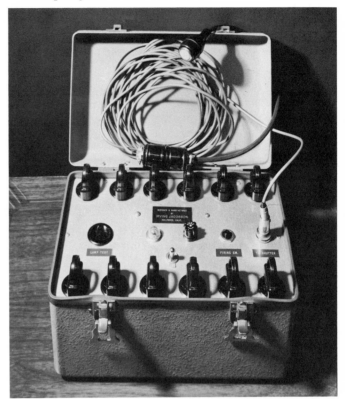

lation of exposure according to the distance of the bulb from the subject and the lens aperture desired for the exposure. Mastering multiple flash exposures is not a simple procedure. Many tests may be necessary before becoming familiar with flash placement and control. Even with careful calculation of exposure, many changes may be desired after it has been tested. Polaroid tests are ideal for fast work.

For color exposures where flash is necessary for interior-exterior light balance, #22B or #50B bulbs should be used. Their high intensity permits use of a small aperture to achieve depth of field and when used with daylight type color film they produce a light value equivalent to that of daylight.

Lighting Techniques

There are essentially two situations encountered in lighting for interior photography. One is where there is no window area so large as to require a balance of indoor and outdoor light. The other is where the window area admits enough light to require balancing. The former situation calls for simple floodlighting and spotlighting equipment for desired effects; the latter calls for the use of flashbulbs.

Where there is not appreciable external light to consider, spotlighting will probably be used to accent textures, forms, etc. This creates dramatic shadow areas which can be softened by floodlights.

Existing artificial light from floor or table lamps and overhead fixtures also create lighting effects. In reality they may be pleasing but photographically they leave areas in shadow. Floodlighting is used to fill these areas also.

The use of floodlights needs careful examination of the interior scene to decide which areas are lacking in brilliance, shadow values, or textures. The floodlights can be placed so as to simulate night or existing light conditions, as required, in conjunction with spotlights. Since floodlights, if uncontrolled, can throw complex and confused shadows and spill into the wrong areas, they should be equipped with barndoors. For instance, too much light often spills out onto the ceiling or the intensity of the flood may destroy soft lighting required in the foreground of a scene. Barndoors will control the direction of the beam.

Floodlights are used to pilot flash lighting set-ups. The area is illuminated by the same procedure as for floodlight exposure except that care must be taken to avoid reflection in glass areas. A warning in the use of flashbulbs. The heat emitted from a flash bulb is great enough to cause a third degree burn. Therefore, after positioning the floodlights in

A photograph can convey the spirit of good living as well as that of good design. Here a multiple flash was used to balance the outdoor light; extreme care was required in setting the lights, for the entire wall separating room from garden terrace is of glass. Light reflections were concealed behind the window columns, a preparation made when using floodlights to pilot the scene. Residence, Los Angeles, California. Jones & Emmons, Architects.

*The soaring heights of free space in
this structure required considerable
auxiliary lighting even to begin
to balance the abundance of daylight
from the glass wall to the left.
Note scale of people on the far left.
Stuart Pharmaceutical Co., Pasadena,
California. Edward D. Stone,
Architect. Thomas D. Church,
Landscape Architect.*

*A lighting technique which is almost
theatrical in its results can
sometimes be used to advantage in
interior photography. Here mushroom
spotlights were carefully placed
to enhance light from existing lamps
and fixtures. Residence, Bel Air,
California. Edward F. White,
Interior Designer.*

*Careful estimate of the exposure
produced a scene with color
values (revealed as tonal values in the
black and white reproduction)
actually superior to those which
would have resulted with bright
sunlight. Originally intended as
a cover photograph for a home
magazine, the picture was later used
for bathing suit advertisements.
Appearances to the contrary, this scene
was taken on a dismal foggy day—
the deadline day; the girls almost froze.
Peggy Sullivan, Landscape Architect.
Courtesy Los Angeles Times.*

Just when it is time to go home (you think) the sun drops into the best position for illuminating the interior of a structure. Here it revealed the texture of furniture and rug. It was not necessary to disturb the "customer" in this industrial lobby. One #22 type flashbulb produced sufficient light to fill shadows. The exposure for this kind of indoor-outdoor scene is the same as that for a straight outdoor composition. Northrop Corporation, Nortonics Division, Palos Verdes, California. Charles Luckman Associates, Architects.

the pilot set-up, remove the light plugs from the wall outlets and plug them into the booster box. The control switch on the box is left in the "off" position until ready. The flood bulbs can then be safely replaced by the flash bulbs. An insulated mitten is a useful item to keep on hand for removing hot bulbs.

Where exterior light is flooding into a room contrasts become very great and the tones on the interior may range from black shadow to brilliant highlights. It would require a huge studio arclight to soften and balance this breadth of light values; the usual spotlights and floodlights are quite inadequate and flashlighting is the only answer.

A single flashbulb fired at the camera position in synchronization with the shutter might produce a fairly good reproduction of a scene. However, it will tend to be flat and will certainly fall short of the quality attainable with more lighting to fill the farthest reaches of the room. Independent flash bulbs carefully placed can give depth and contrast to a scene. The light closest to the camera should be soft so as not to overexpose the foreground; a smaller flash bulb can be used or the reflector can be directed at the ceiling to reflect softly on foreground objects. If the ceiling is dark or too high, a sheet of white material (even a shirt!) can be slung overhead in the right position.

The purpose of flashlighting is seldom to overpower the external light penetrating a scene since this is usually attractive enough to warrant retention. Flash is most often used to soften shadows created by external light so as to reproduce a quality akin to that perceived by the naked eye.

The pictures overleaf were taken from opposite ends of the same room. In the upper one, with sunlight pouring into the room, advantage was taken of the dramatic shadow angle. Exactly the opposite effect was obtained in the lower one which was taken within a few minutes of the other but with backlighting. In both photographs fill light from flashbulbs served to illuminate the shadowed areas. The great contrast between bright sunlight and shadows called for a low-contrast, medium speed film. No. 22-type flashbulbs were used and placed as indicated by the guide number of the bulb and by the fact that an f/32 aperture was needed for good depth of focus. A smaller bulb such as a #11 size would not have given sufficient light, particularly with the dark wood areas in the scenes. Stronger bulbs should also be used where it is not possible to place the lights close to the area to be lit and they must transmit light across a room.

Mid-day overhead sunlight fills this outdoor room with brilliance. Multiple flash illuminated the dark areas where required. Residence, West Los Angeles, California. Cliff May, Designer. Courtesy House & Garden, Condé Nast Publications.

Other procedures than the one described for these illustrations are, of course, possible. However, this is a good working method when time cannot be spared to try out others.

Basically, the exposure for an indoor/outdoor scene is determined by the accuracy with which the outdoor area is to be portrayed. For example, the average exterior, if the sun is bright and a medium yellow filter is being used, requires a medium speed film exposure of about f/32 and 1/10th seconds. To balance this reading the flash determination must be accurate. At first test exposures should be made, varying the distance of the lights from the scene. In this way the exact effect of each flash bulb can be examined.

When shooting interiors with draperies drawn sunlight often produces a strong, glaring pattern on them. Flash should be used to eliminate this even though no exterior view is visible.

A note on stroboscopic lighting. Strobe units derive their light by the discharge of a high voltage current through a gas-filled tube. It is a system used extensively in the studio for portrait, fashion, and other commercial subjects, particularly fast action ones. However, since a single strobe light cannot penetrate so well as a single flash especially in color exposures requiring small lens apertures and synchronized shutter speeds, and since each strobe light requires its own power unit, the battery of lights that would be necessary for architectural lighting would add up to several hundred pounds of equipment—an impossibility for on-location work.

The use of flashlighting for interior color work falls into the same pattern as black and white. Regardless of the type of film used its basic outdoor exposure must be attained with interior flash. Daylight color film is used with blue flash bulbs, usually 50B or 3B types. For small areas #22B can be used.

There is a tendency among professional photographers to use only the so-called existing light in taking their pictures. The greatest drawback to this method is its lack of true visual values and its failure to convey the design being photographed. One often sees interior photographs in which the light from the exterior is completely over-exposed because the photographer has exposed for the interior light values without any supplementary lighting and allowed the exterior light to fall where it may. This results in a glaring news type of photography which is being accepted by a few publications. It is actually a lazy method of photography. As we are trying to stress, it is of utmost importance that the photog-

Whether shooting into the sun as in the lower picture, or away from it as in the upper, the photographer must study the light intensities of flashbulbs so as to understand clearly their effective value in softening strong shadows without producing conflicting tones. The basic exposure here was determined by the light values from the sun streaming into the room. Small #11 type flashbulbs were used in the reflections to diminish the glare of sunlight in the breakfast table setting. Residence, La Jolla, California. Killingsworth, Brady & Smith, Architects.

*The same scene, the upper photograph
taken with existing light only, the lower with
supplementary light. In the first a large window in
the foreground introduced light for the
dining area. A similar window on the left in
the living area and light from the entry door plus
the room lamps provided the remaining
illumination. In the second picture note how
the introduction of spots and floods have provided
a separation of furniture by strengthening
its forms. The shorter exposure thus required
subdued the intensity of the daylight in
the foreground and on the left.*

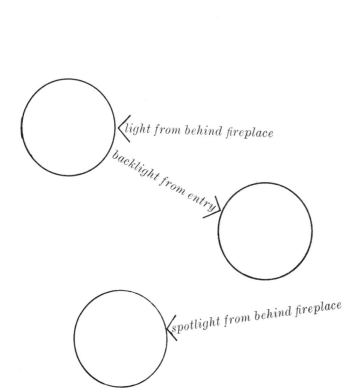

light from behind fireplace

backlight from entry

spotlight from behind fireplace

A complex multiple exposure with existing room lights controlled individually during the exposure was used in this photograph. Because of photographic limitations a direct print from the original negative of this photograph was not desirable. Photographing into the western sky shortly after sunset with a prolonged exposure had destroyed the residual tones. They were restored in the darkroom. Residence, Palm Springs, California. Richard J. Neutra, Architect.

rapher accept responsibility for conveying the design concept. If the light outside a window is so glaring in the exposure that one cannot discern details of exterior design or landscaping or even, on occasion, the interior, what is the point of taking the photograph in the first place?

It is not always necessary to use flash when light balancing is required. This can be achieved by waiting until the sun sets. With flood and spotlights set in advance the exposure is made when the exterior and interior light is of the same intensity. This can be determined by taking an exposure meter reading of the interior and then keeping a check of the exterior values until both interior and exterior balance.

Twilight Black and White

This method of exposure can be used to get effective twilight scenes and the scenes can be from the exterior as well as from the interior. The photograph (opposite) of the desert residence by architect Richard J. Neutra is from this type of exposure. The exposure was begun when the twilight in the sky was waning. Lights in the house were turned out one at a time after allowing for proper exposure for each. The shutter had been set on "bulb," permitting opening and closing at will. This photograph has been published in scores of books and magazines throughout the world. It illustrates much of the drama and beauty of contemporary architecture.

Where twilight scenes are required floodlamps should be arranged and set well in advance of the twilight period for this moment is so fleeting that darkness often sets in before a second exposure can be taken.

Night pictures are not taken at night, primarily because against the background of black sky there is no separation of roof outline. There is also an absence of reflected fill light on surfaces of the building not artificially illuminated. This results in a vague and spotty effect. Examination of the photographs will reveal detail in almost all areas together with a feeling for the mood of the environment.

Twilight Color

This procedure is even more effective when working with color for at twilight the sky reproduces with surprisingly beautiful color qualities. Daylight film should be used and interior areas flashed with blue bulbs. This is necessary for a prolonged exposure of existing floor lamps and other lighting will result in an over-all yellowish color.

The scene to be taken should be studied for dark areas not illuminated by the existing lighting. All the lamps, after testing position with a floodlamp, are run to the camera or

Not a lunar landscape but a house in the Arizona desert whose interior may be seen on page 44. To silhouette the mountains most effectively a late twilight exposure was chosen. Floodlight was used to illuminate the dome. "Burning in" of the sky in the darkroom completed the effect. Residence, Arizona desert. Soleri & Mills, Architects.

The calmness of a twilight scene best displays some architectural elements.
Miramar Chapel, Miramar Naval Air Station, San Diego, California. Richard J.
Neutra, Architect.

72

*This example of contemporary office building design is a glistening gem at
night. Mile-High Center, Denver, Colorado. I. M. Pei, Architect.*

73

This building, standing as it does in water, was an intriguing photographic challenge.

The "night" exposure was taken at twilight to outline the building form and retain detail. Long Beach Water Department Administration Building, Long Beach, California. Heusel, Homolka Associates, Architects.

Bold skeletal structural forms read best when viewed x-ray fashion. This can be achieved only at twilight. Here supplementary floodlighting was used on the interior; darkroom manipulation restored proper tone to sky. Residence, Montecito, Santa Barbara, California. Richard J. Neutra, Architect.

A triad of forms: photographers can find challenging exercises in recording the works of creative architects. Guggenheim Museum, New York, N.Y. Frank Lloyd Wright, Architect.

Here is a demonstration of the extremes which may arise in actual work. Above, left, is shown an over-exposed garden scene; the print value for the interior is normal. In the lower left print the garden was "burned in" to restore the visual quality; this made the interior too dark. The third step, above, is the final version in which light values have been restored to the interior. Residence, San Bernardino, California. Richard J. Neutra, Architect.

to a position within the building where an assistant can fire them. Flash bulbs, either 50B or 22B, are placed in the reflectors. The first exposure should be taken while there is just enough light in the sky to insure a separation of the roof line and to register its color. This exposure may vary from one or two seconds at approximately f/22 to a minute or two, depending upon the prevailing atmospheric conditions. The flashbulbs can be set off any time during the sky exposure. If a longer exposure for the sky is needed, particularly if it has become darker after the first exposure, be certain to turn off bright lights in the building to avoid their over-exposure; the lens can be capped while an assistant does this. If a house is to be photographed and a fireplace is visible, burn a few sheets of twisted newspaper for a glowing effect.

The twilight color composition is one of the most favored among magazine editors since the evening mood is an appealing one. This is true for all types of buildings.

The camera can encompass all the moods of a building, day or night, interior and exterior. The night views on pages 82 and 83 of a living room in Hollywood Hills with a dazzling expanse of lights as far as the eye can see probably serves to convey the feel of this particular location in all its spirit and drama far better than any photograph taken in the daytime could.

Dramatization in lighting is most important in architectural photography and it often spells the difference between a photograph which has impact and one that is just dull. Concentration and experience ultimately lead to such an understanding of lighting possibilities that the photographer can anticipate results even before setting his lights. It is suggested that the illustrations throughout this book be carefully analyzed by the reader to discover how each scene was illuminated.

Darkroom Manipulation

Regardless of conditions on location it is possible, through skillful darkroom manipulation, to control the tonal values of a print during the enlarging process.

The negative may, for example, be devoid of any gradation of sky tones. By exposing while shading the light from the enlarger with the hands the more opaque portions of the negative will transmit more light to restore deeper sky tones to the print. For a blacker sky tone the negative must be removed from the enlarger. With the lens stopped down and the light controlled with the hands as described above, it is

These two pictures indicate the difference between a "straight" print and one dodged to reduce glare and to soften excessive contrasts. Values of surfaces can be restored to realistic tones. Residence, Beverly Hills, California. William Sutherland Beckett, Architect.

A three-dimension effect can be achieved in black and white photography by producing tonal effects in printing. In this case darkroom "paving" of the street with a new surface of blacktop and shading of the sky produced an appealing visual rendering of this unassuming structure. Architect's Office Building, Brentwood Village, West Los Angeles, California. Thornton M. Abell, Architect.

As if suspended in space, this cliff house in the Hollywood Hills has a breathtaking view over Los Angeles. Both pictures were taken within a few minutes of each other with precisely the same lighting set-up. To photograph this scene a disposition of lights was necessary which would not reflect in the walls of glass. As the picture on page 99 shows, the furniture was arranged especially for this composition for the house was new and had not yet been furnished. The furniture and accessories were delivered that same afternoon and placed at the disposal of the photographer. All the preparation was done well before sunset since timing for a twilight photograph, particularly a color one, is very critical. The sky loses color quickly.

The girls were placed and the exposure for the city lights was made, approximately 5 minutes

at f/22, while the girls sat in darkness. The pre-set lights had been fitted with #50B blue flashbulbs. Just before they were flashed for the interior effect the girls assumed their poses for the photograph and the hanging fixtures were turned on.

A house of this type and in this setting can best be portrayed by showing and even featuring its site relationship in a realistic photographic composition. Although this photograph may appear complex in technique it is a straightforward adaptation of a photographic vocabulary.

Awarded first prize in the American Institute of Architects 1960 National Award Competition for Architectural Photography. Residence, Hollywood Hills, California. Pierre Koenig, Architect. Van Keppel-Green, Interiors. Color picture courtesy Holiday Magazine.

In this photograph of an architectural model a black background offered the best means of separation of the gem-like quality of the structure from its surroundings. Model photography requires attention to scale and texture lighting and background control for maximum separation of values is required. Crystal Chapel. Bruce Goff, Architect.

possible to produce any desired sky tone by exposing the sky portion of the paper to the direct light from the enlarger. This takes much time and patience to learn but the accompanying photographs will demonstrate how worthwhile it is.

There are occasions when the paving of old streets is broken and the irregularity of the surface is not an attractive foreground. For the sake of a good composition, since it is not always possible to crop the foreground, careful flashing can re-pave the broken-down street. For this job it is advisable to cut a cardboard template so that the line of the street can more nearly approximate the junction with the curb line.

Careful dodging or flashing of interior scenes can infuse tonal qualities to large expanses of ceilings or floors. Darkening the corners of photographs helps to maintain pictorial impact.

Almost every picture in the author's darkroom receives these kinds of treatment. Maximum visual and reproduction qualities are the purpose of picture taking and darkroom techniques are as much a part of the photographic process as is clicking the camera shutter. The perfectionist should therefore feel no qualms about using the darkroom as much as possible.

The architectural model industry is a thriving one. Almost every firm which designs large structures and developments has models made for study, publicity and client's edification. It is therefore worth discussing architectural model photography as a specialized technique, which it is. Much of it is equally applicable to the photography of industrial design products and of smaller elements in interior design, as well as of art in general.

The photography of models requires primarily a non-conflicting background. This can be any non-textured surface, preferably a neutral tone for black and white work. For color the photographer should use a roll of blue paper to approximate sky values. If a landscaped area is available, careful composing can give a realistic quality to the model.

Because most models are of greatly reduced scale, it is often difficult to achieve low angle or ground level views. This problem can be avoided by experimenting with various focal length lenses. In some instances, although a wide angle lens depth of focus is desirable, too much foreground is attained. On the other hand, a long focal length lens is

In photographing an architectural model it is possible to simulate evening illumination; interior lighting of the model adds to its realistic appearance. Small flood and spot lights have been used here to emphasize separation between units. Model of Barrington Plaza, West Los Angeles, California. Daniel, Mann, Johnson, & Mendenhall, Architects & Engineers.

The whole is the summation of its parts. Pictures of minute elements of machinery are sometimes required in industrial photographs. In them lighting must help render the form and material of small parts.

Industrial photography must speak the language of the engineer and scale, as shown here by the operator, is extremely important. Supplementary floodlighting created highlights and backlighting effects in this photograph. American Airlines Jet Operational & Maintenance Building, Tulsa, Oklahoma. Coston, Frankfurt & Short, Architects & Engineers.

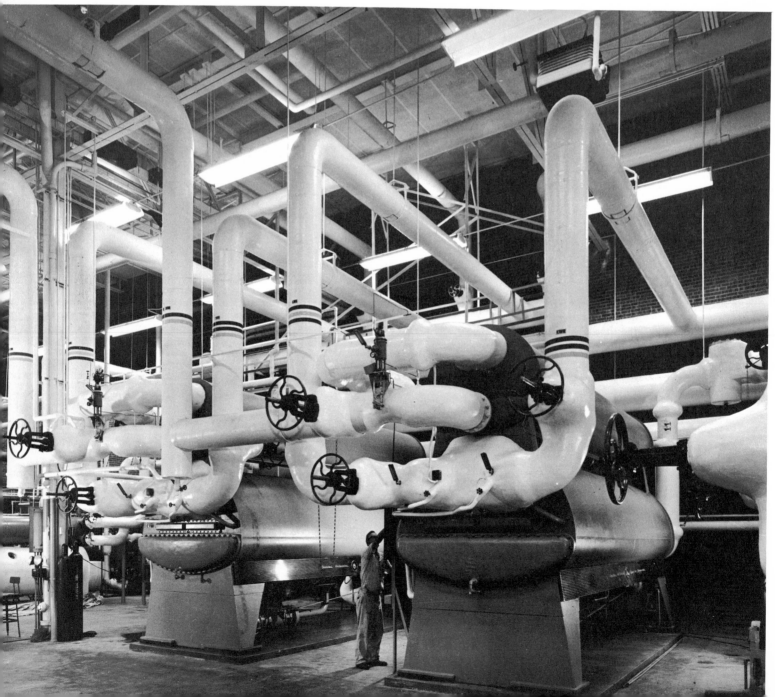

For complete plant coverage, a close-up of typical activity is desirable. Depth of focus is of no particular advantage in this type of scene so it was taken at f/8, 1/50 seconds on medium speed film. A supplementary 350-watt mushroom spot bulb was used for backlighting the subject. American Electronics, Inc., Fullerton, California. Eugene K. Choy, Architect.

equally undesirable because of its compressing of perspective which produces a box-like proportion. Wherever possible, therefore, a medium focal length lens is best. Each model, according to its scale will have its own photographic characteristics. The photographer must study the plan and scale of the structure in order to understand the optical requirements fully. For most purposes a low angle, slightly above roof top perspective is best.

To simulate the brilliance and shadow quality of sunlight in the studio, a spotlight should provide the primary source. Care should be taken in supplementary fill light so as to avoid confusing shadows. One way of accomplishing this is to aim the fill light towards a dull reflecting surface, a wall or ceiling if light-toned will do. Supported on a stand, the reflector can be turned so as to direct the "bounce" or reflected light to exactly the desired intensity into the spotlight's shadows. Be certain that the lights have barndoors for complete control.

Some models have ingenious interior lighting. This is a boon to the photographer for, with a few low intensity spotlights, a structure can be made to assume a realistic appearance.

On night scenes of a model, two or three light sources are permissible, simulating existing area lighting. These lights can back-light the face of a wall or strongly cross-light a textured garden or deck area.

For a thorough study of lighting, models should be set on a turntable. A slight turn is often enough competely to change an effect. Lights should be solidly supported. A clutch device should be fixed to the turntable shaft.

Model photography is a great challenge. Some photographers have been acclaimed for their prowess in creating fantastically realistic compositions. It can even become a specialty for there is a constant demand for good photography of models.

Industrial Photography
Industrial photography as it pertains to in-plant activities is most frequently involved in equipment, production, and technical illustrations. This requires interiors of facilities and equipment, together with the general coverage of exteriors.

Photography of industrial interiors, particularly those containing large items, must be done with attention to scale

The brilliant illumination of most industrial plants makes possible unposed "activity" photographs. This one was at f/16, 1/10 seconds, with fast film, and camera back and front swings adjusted for increased depth. American Electronics, Inc., Fullerton, California. Eugene K. Choy, Architect.

and careful illustration of activity. Too often in photographs the industrial operator overpowers the more dramatic machine on which he is working. The opposite is preferable, and even a pair of hands may be sufficient indication of the presence of a person and his size relative to the machine. Where the photograph is to be of operational activity, unless a specific personality is to be photographed, care should be taken to avoid the perennial "mug shot." The operator doing the mugging may lose a hand in the process!

Scale and lighting are the key to good industrial compositions. The scale can be realized by adroit framing with associated equipment and the use of familiar objects to relate to the operation being performed.

The tendencies to use existing lighting or flashlighting on the camera should be avoided. Miniature reflectors with small flashbulbs will provide more than ample lighting for most scenes of average size. The sparkle and drama of industrial operation photographs are derived from back lighting.

Landscape Photography

Photography of landscaping is not unlike that of interior design. The good landscape architect designs his structural elements—paving, screen, planted areas—in direct relationship to the building. This the photographer should recognize and illustrate with a keen observation of natural lighting effects on textures of plant material and other physical elements of the design.

It is good to be able to recognize species of plants and to become familiar with their photogenic qualities. Garden and landscape editors often need identification of plant material and a photographer covering a project for possible publication performs an appreciated service if he gives all this information to the editors in as complete a package as possible.

The designer or other amateur architectural photographer will usually be photographing exteriors or interiors in their existing state except, perhaps, for simple lighting effects and the flick of a duster here or there. The professional, however, has a little further to go. Since he is so much more concerned with illustrations of design for public or client consumption, his range of knowledge must be broader than that which one would normally associate with photography. The following text is intended mainly for the professional photographer although the designer himself can read it with profit; from

American industry has accepted the architect's concept of introducing park-like (and almost country club) environment in its plants. This being so, industrial photographers are well-advised to learn at least the rudiments of architectural composition so as to be able to capture architectural forms of the plant. American Electronics, Inc., Fullerton, California. Eugene K. Choy, Architect.

The old swimming hole has become part of the landscape architect's design requirements. Here a pool was located in a rocky setting. The photograph, taken from roof height, displays the form and setting. A ball tossed into the water highlighted the quiet surface with ripples. Residence, Palm Springs, California. Williams & Williams, Architects.

90

The fuzz of festuca is best shown with backlighting.
This composition was predicated on texture and relationship
to other elements in the garden. Residence, Arcadia,
California. Burton A. Schutt, Architect.

The dynamic force of structure frames this landscape.
Taken in the soft light at dusk, no extraneous shadows or
highlights interfere with the quiet mood. Residence,
Los Angeles, California. Richard J. Neutra, Architect.

Here (left) in the Arizona desert is a blend of architectural and natural landscape. This photograph was taken with infra-red film to lighten the red rock masses and to emphasize the delicate clouds; it was composed to encompass both chapel and setting. Chapel of the Holy Cross, Sedona, Arizona. Anshen & Allen, Architects.

Interpretive use of infra-red film in the scene at lower left has helped define tree forms and the design of the planted area. Residence, Palm Springs, California. Williams & Williams, Architects.

Small garden design can be picturesque. A trellis hidden by foliage is revealed in the photograph by its shadow. Time of day was selected especially to get effective reflections on the water. Fill flash was used in the same direction as the sunlight to diffuse heavy shadows. Residence, Bel Air, Los Angeles, California. Eckbo, Dean & Williams, Landscape Architects.

it he will derive some idea of what his photographer must do to get the photographs he desires and also get some pointers for taking professional-looking photographs himself.

The best procedure for the complete photographing of a building is to arrange for a prior inspection by the photographer. On this visit he can note the placement of the building in relation to its neighbors; he can note lighting conditions (by time chart, if necessary) and what supplementary lighting may be necessary; he can note possible camera locations and angles for the best interpretation of the design elements with which he is primarily concerned; he can decide which camera, lens, film, etc. will best accomplish this interpretation; and he can note any "dressing up" which may be necessary (eg. if its landscaping is not yet completed, he may decide that a few extra plants would enhance an exterior picture of a building).

It is advisable to study weather conditions before going out on an exterior assignment, particularly one that is at all distant; driving or flying several hundreds of miles only to find oneself in the middle of a three-day rainstorm can be very frustrating, not to say costly. The weather bureau publishes charts daily in most newspapers. Television stations have excellent weather reportage, complete with "hot and cold Isobars" and charts indicating weather fronts and barometric pressures; it is worthwhile learning their vocabularies. Specific local and up-to-the-minute weather can be checked by telephone from the nearest airport weather service or from local newspaper reports. This information, carefully followed, can save unnecessary trips, ensure that correct equipment is taken, and help plan a more efficient work routine.

On architectural and interior design assignments it is often necessary for the photographer to provide props and accessories, either exterior or interior, or both.

When a building must for some reason be photographed before landscaping has grown, a few additional shrubs and trees in cans or pots can be carefully placed to fill in the bare spots. Here a knowledge of plant material comes in handy for sparse growth can be supplemented with a few naturally placed branches to frame a scene. Bring a few pine boughs from your own garden—or your neighbor's. Illustrated is a scene done for a prominent national publication where a sparse condition was remedied, complete with roses! The walnut branches were "pruned" from the trees behind the house and the roses were borrowed from a nursery. (Keep cutters and garden shears among your tools.)

An exploratory visit with small camera (Hasselblad Superwide) to this drive-in bank revealed the possibility of supplementary night photography desirable to avoid a disturbing background. Compare the day and night scenes for clarity of structural forms and textural qualities. Central National Bank, Drive-In Branch, Oklahoma City, Oklahoma. Wright & Selby, Architects.

Beverages are not the only things subject to instant preparation as is evident from the photograph at top left, though not from the final photographs (below) which were an assignment for Good Housekeeping magazine. The portable garden was also used in the patio of the same house, as shown below. Residence, West Covina, California. Cliff May, Builder. Chris Choate, Architect.

The barren landscaping (upper right) of a church has been improved with a few carefully placed branches. The "trees" (lower right) were actually small branches cut from a neighboring elm and placed over the camera on supporting light stands. This device takes very little time and can improve a photographic scene. Riviera Methodist Church, Hollywood Riviera, California. Richard J. Neutra, Architect.

The open doors of the cabinets, the makings of a salad, and decorative glass accessories provide a decorative touch to a kitchen photograph. They also provide color accents in a color photograph. Note the separation between the center island and other areas of the kitchen; the light was placed on the floor and reflected from a white dish towel. Residence, Beverly Hills, California. William Stephenson, Architect. Courtesy House & Garden, Condé Nast Publications.

Housekeeping occupies a significant place on the list of photographers' "musts." It has even been known for the photographer to furnish an empty house where pictures were needed in a hurry! However, things are not usually this bad and the photographer's housekeeping problems are more likely to be on a smaller scale. Whether doing a home, an office, or a lobby, all cushions have to be tidy and arranged; draperies, if partly drawn, should have the folds uniform and straight; lamp shades must not be askew and lamp cords can easily be taped to back table legs to eliminate conspicuous wires. If there are decorative house plants, be sure to turn them for their best profile. Coffee and lamp tables are often cluttered with untidy stacks of magazines and odds and ends in the form of ash trays, bowls, flowers, and even last night's highball glasses. These must be tidied up or, better still, cleared away because accessories should be kept to a minimum to avoid overcrowding and destroying form by the spotty appearance of many small objects. Two or three objects of good shape and proportion to the table size are usually adequate. In many instances a book, a low formal flower arrangement, and an ash tray produce the best results.

Table setting scenes may require the preparation of food items—such as tossed salad—and God help the photographer with no domestic talents!

After continuous tramping back and forth on carpeting, footsteps are conspicuous and the nap of the carpet is uneven. When all is in readiness a quick vacuuming or brushing will restore the texture and tonal values. This apparently obvious chore is often overlooked by both editors and photographers.

In kitchens the photographer must exercise his ingenuity. The monotony of expanses of sink and work areas can be relieved by a few lived-in items. Near the sink, for example, can be a casual arrangement of vegetables for a salad. A salad bowl, tools and condiments can be near by. Or, if illustrating a bake center in a kitchen, an arrangement of appropriate utensils, a bowl of eggs, mixing bowl, measuring equipment, and even some apples for a pie produce an attractive working atmosphere. And the photogenic artichoke or the halved cabbage can always be relied upon to produce desirable textures. Anyone for eggplant?

Photographers are often called upon to produce publicity and sales material for tract house developments. With meager accessorization, the photographer must stretch his resources to make the often minimum size rooms look lived-in. Certain

This Arts and Architecture Case Study house was not furnished at the photography deadline date and furniture had to be supplied specifically for the assignment. The color and black and white pictures on pages 82 and 83 show how the house appeared that same night. Arts & Architecture Case Study House, Los Angeles, California. Pierre Koenig, Architect. Van Keppel-Green, Interiors.

The sparkle of light on even fairly ordinary glass and crockery is a gleaming foreground for a kitchen photograph. Depth of focus was sufficient to give a good idea of the setting of the kitchen in the architecture of the house. Residence, Bel Air, Los Angeles, California. Harold W. Leavitt, Architect; Ernest W. LeDuc, Associate Architect. Courtesy House & Garden, Condé Nast Publications.

Models should be used with great care in architectural photography: the architectural design is the important element of the photograph; disturbing, outdated fashions and overpowering human forms are merely distracting and have no importance. Therefore, placement should be based on normal scale and for demonstration of architectural elements. General Dynamics Astronautics, San Diego, California. Charles Luckman Associates, William L. Pereira Associates, Architects.

A warm mood of young people's activity—a family room without family would be a waste of photographic and editorial effort. Extension flash lighting was strung throughout the extensive area, having first been piloted with floodlight bulbs. Seven lights were used in the flash exposure in order to create a feeling of existing lighting and to stop the action which had been developed in rehearsal. The exposure of f/32, 1/10 seconds was fast enough to stop movement. Residence, West Los Angeles, California. Cliff May, Designer. Courtesy House & Garden, Condé Nast Publications.

Here is another unposed "action" photograph: a native potter in Yucatan; note the stack of raw clay to the right. Natural lighting from windows and door was used unsupplemented.

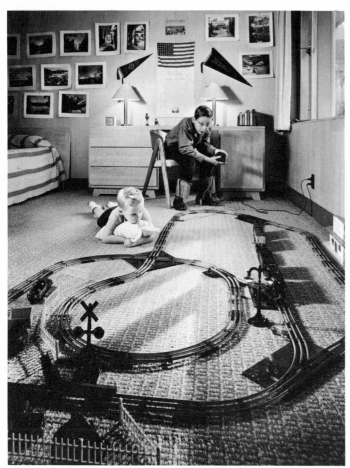

The fascination of model railroading is here portrayed with a low camera angle and great depth of field, the latter produced by tilting the lens board forward. Floodlights provided supplementary lighting. The scene was not posed; flash was used and exposure taken at f/32, 1/50 seconds, while the train was running. Residence, Beverly Hills, California. Ulysses Floyd Rible, Allison & Rible, Architects.

items should be requested so that they can be placed to produce a better photograph than so many of those published in Sunday real estate supplements. Many builders have to depend upon the photographer's directions, so a check list should be part of the equipment for the job. Accessories are usually needed for almost every room.

Although architectural photography is looked upon with some misgivings by certain editors concerned with "life" in their photography, live models are often used by photographers. It requires careful study, however, for unless models appear in spontaneous action scenes seem stilted. People in architectural photographs are useful for showing scale and activity. However, they should not be placed so close to the camera as to become overpowering and ponderous in the composition. There is a great danger of cluttering up a view with a half dozen people sprawled all over the couches and chairs in a room. Certainly most viewers of the photograph are not interested in seeing a group of people preempting the scene. A wise photographer will find ways of handling composition so that live subjects will enhance the architectural scene without becoming too conspicuous. A garden with a couple walking in the distance might make a pleasant composition. But place the same two people close to the camera digging up petunias—and you have a scene of two people digging up petunias, that's all.

An important rule to follow in the photography of any building is to be certain that no one is staring at the camera when the photographs are being taken. The purpose of having people in the picture is to imply that this is an actual activity and nothing ruins such a composition more than, say, a group of children in a classroom looking right into the lens, or a group of workers on a job posing for the camera rather than paying attention to what they are supposed to be doing. Spontaneous action is the prerequisite!

In photographing children's rooms it is usually desirable to create a warm and congenial atmosphere with a feeling that children really do use the room. However, it would be advisable first to photograph a cleaned-up area in spic and span condition with a view camera. Then allow the children in; let them begin to play with their toys and proceed to photograph them candidly with a small camera. Both types of scenes are then available for use. This type of coverage provides photographs for both architectural magazines which are primarily concerned with formal design shots and home service magazines seeking human interest activity in rooms.

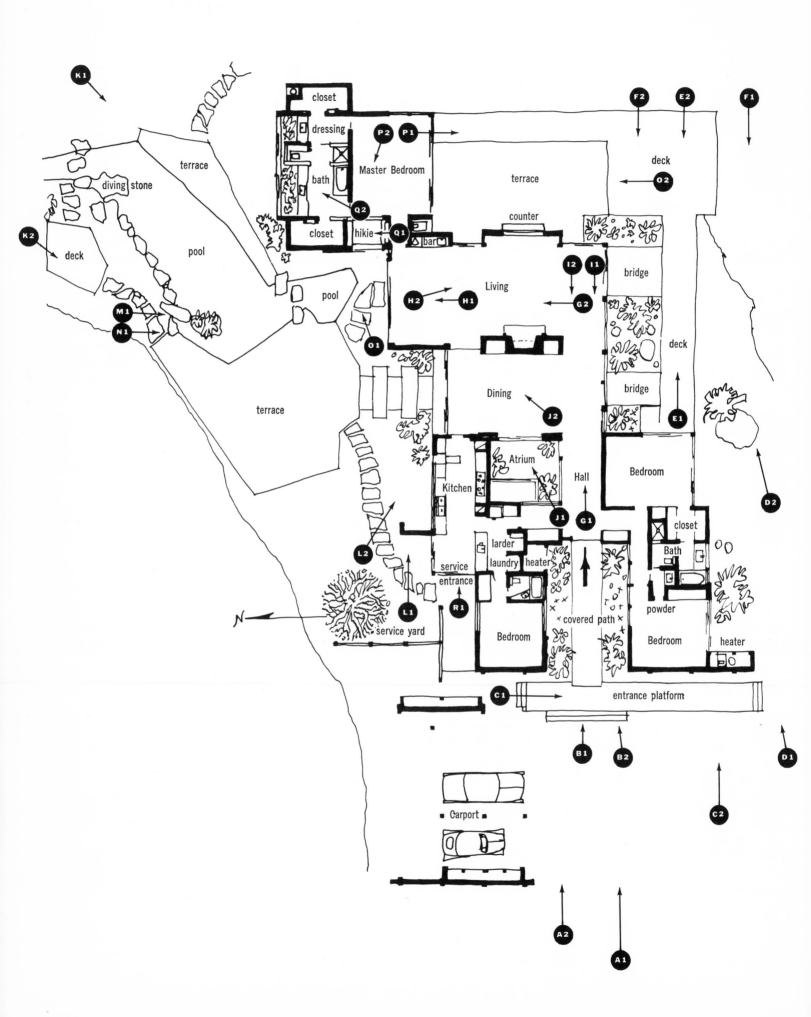

K1

F2   E2   F1

closet

dressing

P2   P1

Master Bedroom

deck

terrace

K2

deck

diving stone

terrace

bath

pool

Q2

counter

O2

closet   hikie

Q1   bar

I2   I1

bridge

pool

H2   H1   Living   G2

deck

M1

N1

O1

bridge

E1

terrace

Dining

J2

Bedroom

D2

Atrium

Kitchen

Hall

J1   G1

closet

L2

larder

Bath

laundry   heater

service
entrance

powder

N

L1

R1

Bedroom

covered path

Bedroom

heater

service yard

C1   entrance platform

B1   B2

D1

C2

Carport

A2

A1

Chapter V   Photographic Case Study

The numbers on this plan of the photographic case study house indicate the camera placement for each of the keyed pictures in the following pages. The arrows show the direction in which the camera was facing in each case. Residence, Bel Air, California. Harold W. Levitt, Architect; Ernest W. Le Duc, Assoc. Architect. Ann Sullivan, Peggy Galloway, Interior Designers. Edward Huntsman-Trout, Landscape Architect.

This chapter is devoted to a photographic study of a residence in Bel Air, Los Angeles, California which was designed by Harold W. Leavitt, Architect with Ernest W. Le Duc as Associate Architect. The primary intent in showing it here is to demonstrate what the photographer must do to make the layout and general feeling of a structure comprehensible to the photographic viewer. The procedure to be followed in such a study can be considered in many ways. Essentially the photographer must understand the requirements of his client, whether a magazine, a designer, or an advertiser.

In this instance the house was selected for publication by *House & Garden* Magazine. The editor reviewed the house with the photographer and presented him with a "script." The photographer was requested to photograph the house under the conditions he felt most suitable for realizing the editorial needs.

Producing photographs by this procedure is much akin to motion picture production because of the sensitive requirements of sunlight and shadow. The editor's precepts must be adhered to but they are not necessarily rigid ones; more often they are general indications of the editorial attitude and the photography does not have to be subjugated or compromised entirely. Rather, the editor would prefer that the photographer interpret his suggestions as guides and not as actual directives.

In this particular house, with its abundance of glass walls providing direct relationship to the exterior areas, the only possible photographic procedure was one making use of fill flash and the flashbulbs' sizes had to be very carefully selected. As many as five or six lights were used in several of these scenes because the dark walls, white carpeting, and white ceilings created great contrasts and it was further necessary to equalize all these values with the exterior brightness. Some areas were deliberately kept dark and others brilliantly highlighted.

This house was published in the July 1961 issue of *House & Garden*. Just how the art director assembled the material is worth study for from it can be deduced the importance placed on certain photographs. Such selections are usually made on the basis of content (as it interests the individual magazine) and the visual impact on the printed page.

The importance of composition in a photograph cannot be over-emphasized. In all the illustrations in this book observe carefully the beginning and end of each photograph. Notice that the eye is not allowed to wander, that each area shown has a specific point of interest, and that the viewer's eyes are literally controlled. This is possible to achieve with lighting emphasis as well as by selection of structural and decorative elements.

Establishment of structure and site is very important. This particular home has a long driveway. It is adjacent to an existing old estate whose garden wall is shown in A1. Placement of people in the middle distance has helped to give scale and animation to the scene. Time of day was extremely important to get the shadows of the structure on the house and the trees across the driveway. This is also true of A2 in which the camera has been moved closer to the house.

B1

B2

The first two photographs were taken with sunlight just crossing the surface of the wall which faced west and required an exposure shortly after noon. The entrance detail in B1 was taken earlier in the day when sunlight was not hitting the west wall directly. This provided a back light quality and enhanced the pictorial aspect of the composition. An extension flash used to soften the shadows at the front entrance area was synchronized with the shutter. By moving the camera to the right an entirely different composition was obtained in B2. The sunlight had moved around to the west and was illuminating the front steps and walls of the house from a different angle. Notice how the beams of the overhang and the columns are more clearly understandable from a design and perspective point of view as compared with B1, taken earlier in the day.

107

The previous photographs did not show well the overhang which protects the front entry and deck of the house. C1, taken from the carport end of the house, clearly illustrates how the roof overhang is supported and the small air space which separates it from the house. This picture was taken with a *Hasselblad Superwide* camera with a 2¼ x 2¼ size negative and from a low angle to capture the form and drama of the structure; it demonstrates that views of this kind can be taken without setting up a large camera on a tripod. In considering the structural and design elements of the front of the house, compare A2 with C2. The former was taken from the driveway, the latter considerably to the right. The architect used the continuation of the overhang along the front of the house to frame the garden approach to its rear.

C1

C2

The architectural use of the overhang is further
illustrated in D1. Here two of the columns and the end
of the overhang form a decorative "gate" to introduce
the viewer to a more dimensional aspect of the garden
entrance. In D2 the framing of the view was
determined by the edge of the wall at the left allowing
the overhang to extend over the walkway and
completing the composition with the dark-toned pine
tree on the right. This view is excellent for
studying the landscape plan and garden treatment
in the design of the steps and the gravel path area.

E1

Walking up the broad steps of D2 the view is of an extended walkway towards the garden deck in the rear. These four photographs show the view in both directions. E2 and F2, while illustrating the same general architectural elements, are quite different from a camera point of view; both should be carefully studied. F2 is perhaps the more inviting because of the foreground emphasis on setting and furnishing detail but lacks the long perspective of E2. F2 gives a glimpse of the living room glass wall to the right; in E2 the camera is further to the left, looking away from that particular area and stressing the deck and over-all framing of the house. F1, a detail for the landscape architect, was one of a series taken with the Hasselblad camera. Notice how clearly discernible is each pebble.

E2

G 1

Inside the front entry (B1) is the scene shown in G1.
The view goes right through to the rear of the house and
looks out through the window visible on the right in F2.
The viewer of the photographs is thus given an opportunity
to orient himself with the plan of the house. Turning
left at the light fixture towards the end of the passageway
in G1 reveals the view of the living room in G2 as it looks out
in an entirely different direction towards the garden
and swimming pool area.

G 2

Closer to the far end of the living room,
H1 shows a detail of the room and its
furnishing in relationship to the swimming
pool and garden area. Most of the previous
photographs were taken with wide angle lenses
but H1 was taken with a normal lens so as to
bring up the garden detail and not force it
back in perspective as a wide angle lens would
have done. This was possible because there
was sufficient room in the large living area for
the camera to be set back far enough to pick up
enough composition without forcing the
perspective as a wide angle lens would have
done. Looking back from the end of the living
room shown in H1 gives the view in H2—
towards the desk and view side of the house.
In both cases auxiliary lighting has been used.
Floodlights were first set up and piloted so
that the lights were positioned to avoid
reflections in the tremendous amount of glass
in this house. Then the floodlights were
replaced with flash and the procedure
described in the lighting section of
Chapter IV was followed.

H2

A photographer cannot photograph only
one side or feature of any area; in
order to be clearly discernible to the
reader the photographs must
portray all the major elements and
relationships so that the plan is
clear. Moving down to the end of the area
shown in G1 and turning about, the view
is as shown in I1 and I2. Again, as
in E2 and F2, the photographer must
decide which elements of a scene
are to be emphasized. The differences
between I1 and I2, although not
great, are still sufficient for clear analysis
to be important.

I1

I2

Moving back to the chest near the entry, shown in I1, the camera has been redirected, this time towards an inner garden court with a view through to the dining area of the house. This is shown in J1. The retention of the chest in this picture (right foreground) helps to orient the viewer to the original scene, G1, looking into the house from the entry. Such anchor points are very important because orientation saves confusion on the part of the viewer. Moving into the scene on the same axis as J1, the dining area, J2, becomes more clearly determined. This time the view looks out towards the rear swimming pool and garden area and, once again, flash balance was developed to distinguish the indoor/outdoor relationship. This type of photography involves considerable care in the placement of lights.

J1

J2

K1

Landscaping photographs must pick out interesting and important design features and should show, in most instances, their relationship to the structure of the building. K1 and K2 illustrate landscape design features like the use of wood in decking and tree well protection, and the rock garden and patio formations. The integration of garden and house have also been demonstrated.

K2

L1

L1 illustrates the rear garden pool area as seen when entering from behind the carport. At first glance the illustration covers a wide area and seems to be quite complete in itself, for it shows the relationship of the structural elements of the house to the garden as climaxed by the large trees on the left. However, by moving in closer to the roof overhang, as in L2, further photographic development of the area's themes is possible. The architectural treatment of the roof and the canvas protection for a dining patio are dramatized.

L2

Some of the more pictorial views possible in the coverage of a house can be obtained at night. The scene
of the pool and its relationship to the living and dining areas of the house shown in M1 and N1 clearly
portrays this type of photography. This scene was taken at twilight before the sky became too dark so as to
delineate the form of the roof against the sky. The color picture was taken shortly before the black
and white since color values become lost in deeper twilight. Auxiliary lighting was used inside the house
to get sufficient light reflection from the ceiling into the pool. The exterior garden lights were supplemented
by small spotlights to illuminate the fascia and beams of the house. Exposure on this scene was
first made with the existing floor lamps and skylight. Then, with the lens covered, auxiliary lights were
placed and another short exposure given to produce the desired effects on the above-mentioned areas.
Even the rock in the foreground had a diffused light cast upon it so as to give better form rendition.

In O1 the camera has been moved in under the overhang shown in the previous picture. In it the glass bedroom wall and shoji sliding screen are emphasized and the swimming pool/garden relationship once again become prominent. This view also illustrates the stepping stones and the gravel garden area. Since there was a dark shaded area in the foreground looking out to bright sunlight, fill flash was necessary; in this case it was from a light placed on the far right of the composition. By synchronizing the flash it was possible to photograph the scene without compromising too much on the intense sunlight hitting the rear garden area.

In O2 the camera has been placed as in E2 but facing 90° to the right. The resulting view is of the rear terrace of the living room looking towards the bedroom wing of the house. Here the draperies have been kept closed so as not to distract attention from the quiet simplicity of the design of this wing.

02

120

In the master bedroom with the draperies open, P1 was taken looking back over the writing desk towards the terrace from which O2 was taken. With the camera behind the writing desk, the bedroom itself is shown more fully in P2. Here the view is towards the rear garden and a glimpse is caught of the lounge chairs and umbrella in the swimming pool area.

Q1

Q2

The lounge area of the bedroom, a retreat designed for reading and relaxation, has been clearly illustrated in Q1. The same area has been shown in the background of P2; the close-up photograph was considered necessary to give the reader more detailed information about its design and construction. In taking Q1 additional lighting, in the form of synchronized flash, was used on the exterior to simulate sunlight—a useful device when it is not possible to take the picture at the time of day ideal for composition. In this house every room is related to some part of the garden and even the bathroom, as shown in Q2, has an intimate view of the rear garden with a glimpse of one end of the swimming pool. Notice the simple arrangement of accessories and the minimally reflected soft light used to balance the exterior sunlight.

122

*R1 is a standard kitchen view. On page 100 (Chapter IV) is a photograph taken
from its far end, back through the opened china closet. In the latter picture the
kitchen has become more visually exciting and the elements still read quite clearly.
The use of concealed backlighting helps to produce clear delineation of
glass and dinner ware, as well as desirable highlights.*

How—and why—does a photographer come to specialize in architectural work? The why can only be answered by the individual—accident, vocation, profit, flair, take your choice. The how is the subject of this chapter; in short form it can be described as diligence, application, interest in design, and sheer hard work with a dash of inspiration for good measure.

There are (perhaps unfortunately) no legal requirements in the United States for entering the profession and it is therefore up to the individual to establish his own standards. Nor do high standards constitute rank idealism; there is a perfectly practical basis for them; it does not take long for an architect or a magazine editor to appreciate whether the work presented is that of an expert or a hack. The establishment of an authoritative background and a good reputation in the field of architectural photography must therefore be carefully sought.

While education in both architecture and photography would obviously form an ideal background, this is seldom possible and there are few, if any, specific courses in architectural photography per se. The usual way into the field is by means of formal schooling or self-training in photography itself and then the acquisition of the necessary background for specialization in architectural photography.

Education and Training

So far as formal education is concerned, there are numerous schools of photography, public and private, throughout the United States. The curricula of many universities as well as those of every major art and design school now offer courses in photography—including photojournalism. In addition there are such special schools as the New York School of Photography, the Art Center School in Los Angeles, as well as many other hundreds of private ones in other cities.

Whereas self-taught photography was common years ago, today's economic conditions necessitate an accelerated learning process. However, it is certainly possible to pick up the fundamentals of photography without formal training provided time is not of the essence. Most libraries and book stores have excellent books on all aspects of photography. These will provide detailed information, will help the beginner to learn basic techniques, and will help both beginner and advanced photographer to learn specialized techniques.

Once a basic formal or self-training program has been completed, the would-be professional photographer is advised to get some experience in as broad a commercial practice as possible. Although it is often facetiously referred to as "nuts and bolts" photography, this work will produce an

The skeletal structure of this chapel is echoed in the pattern of sunlight and shadows. The photographic exposure for this scene is the same as it would be for an exterior. Dark areas were carefully illuminated with flash which was kept subdued so as not to interfere with the natural effect. Wayfarers' Chapel, Palos Verdes, California. Lloyd Wright, Architect.

understanding of composition, lighting, and lens and camera effects and controls in many situations. By involving himself in commercial practice the beginner will learn to master the often complex manipulations of the view camera.

After this, once he has become thoroughly versed in the elementary procedures of photography, the beginner is best advised to apprentice himself to an established worker in architectural photography. Even on a part-time basis, and no matter how difficult it is to find, training so gained is valuable. There is no regular apprenticeship system in architectural photography yet professional photographers should accept the responsibility for passing on their knowledge to the next generation.

The alternative to apprenticeship is self-training in architectural photography. The fundamental requirement is sensitivity to the thinking and intention of the creative designer. This does not imply a literal reproduction of design elements on photographic film. It implies, rather, an interpretive approach to the photography of structure so that its visual appeal will be positive. The 8 x 10 glossy print lying on the architect's table should satisfy him that the photographer has realized (in the deepest sense) the intent, nature, and purpose of the design. Conversely, the potential client who is studying the photograph of the architect's design should be able to grasp the significance of the structure being viewed. It is only by much thought and experience that a photographer can learn to interpret design elements intelligently. We are here outlining a possible program of self-training the details of which will, naturally, be a purely personal matter for each individual.

One approach is to study all available magazines and books in which architectural photographs appear. From them a careful analysis of camera angles, perspectives, and lighting used in interior and exterior photographs—day and night—should be made. Each photograph should be judged to determine what the photographer was trying to accomplish. Years of perseverance and practice of this kind will give facility in this respect.

Whenever possible a photographer should work with the architect or designer on location. The two can then discuss the subject to be photographed and the designer's viewpoint can be clarified for the photographer in job after job until it becomes practically second nature to the photographer. In addition, it is often possible that the designer can precisely define his feelings about his design and thus enable the photographer to avoid featuring elements which may not be important in reporting the building. A word of warning however: the designer's viewpoint should not always be taken too literally; often he knows little about photography and his opinions should be interpreted in photographic terms rather than followed specifically.

Another excellent method is to visit a building armed with published photographs (someone else's). Before looking at the photographs, one's own should be taken for comparison—some Polaroid snapshots will give quick results for examination on the spot. In the comparison of one's own pictures with those of the published photographer, much can be learned about technique and the development of the seeing eye. This form of analysis is both constructive and challenging and tends to minimize the tendency to copy another photographer's style in that one becomes very much aware of that style.

Another possible method of training an architectural photographer is one that has not yet been used. It would require cooperation among the architects and designers themselves and would be particularly appropriate in those parts of the country where there is a shortage of architectural photographers. Local architects and other designers (perhaps through their professional organizations, the American Institute of Architects, the American Institute of Interior Designers, the National Society of Interior Designers, or some combination of these organizations) would appoint a committee which would invite local photographers to discuss architectural photography. Slides and magazine photographs could be shown and the discussion held to analyze the pictures taken by the photographers present. This might be the first step toward a program of improving architectural photography. It may seem a long and tortuous method but unless architects and other design professionals take the matter in hand there is little likelihood of improvement on the part of the photographers upon whom they are forced by circumstances to rely. It would, therefore, behoove the architects and designers to teach the photographers the basic elements of design particularly from the camera-eye view. This does not mean the designer needs to become a photographic expert but that he become conscious of the photographic possibilities of the design elements. Certainly a designer can recognize whether a building looks better from a high or low angle, for example. He can tell whether it looks better from a one point elevation of from an extreme foreshortened wide angle view

The upper photograph has been taken with a view
down the nave—the orthodox angle in church photography.
The lower photograph is more informative of interesting
design details such as the curved ceiling, the sconces,
and the altar arrangement. *First Presbyterian Church,
Cottage Grove, Oregon. Pietro Belluschi, Architect.*

looking down the length of the façade. If architects can learn to think this way they can discuss photography more intelligently with the photographer as well as helping a non-specialist photographer in the intricacies of photographing architecture and architectural interiors.

Photographic Organizations

Three major photographic organizations exist and each is of some interest to the architectural photographer. The largest commercial organization is the Professional Photographers of America, Incorporated (PPA, Inc.). This organization, although devoted to the activities of the commercial photographer, has much to offer to the beginner in architectural photography, for the organization is so vast that its program covers all kinds of photographic activity. It also establishes procedures and ethics as well as carrying on an extensive research on the business organization of photographic studios. This can be a tremendous help to the beginner.

The American Society of Magazine Photographers (ASMP) is composed of photographers who devote the bulk of their time to magazine work. Although not many beginning photographers would be eligible for membership, associate membership is available for a limited period to beginners just getting into specialized work in the magazine field. The ASMP has for many years been in the forefront in the development of ethical codes for magazine work. It is through the efforts of this association that the standards of magazine photography have been raised to such high levels, especially during the last decade. Although most of the membership of the ASMP work for general magazines, a large number of the membership does work in the architectural field as well.

The third and most immediately logical organization for the architectural photographer is the Architectural Photographers Association (APA). This association is composed entirely of specialists in the architectural and design fields and its work is primarily concerned with establishing codes and ethics for the architectural photographer just as the ASMP does for magazine photographers in general. It also attempts to study and analyze the relationship of photographers with architects, commercial users of photography, publishers, and editors. The APA also works closely with various organizations in promoting public relations for the membership as well as arranging exhibits of members' work. The APA has worked closely with the American Institute of Architects and has collaborated in arranging travelling exhibits of the best architectural photography.

Constructive work towards the betterment of photographic standards, business as well as esthetic, is constantly being done by all three of these organizations. One, two, or all three can be joined with profit if only to meet one's fellow professionals.

Rights and Fees

In ordinary commercial photography a customer may order a photograph and a set of prints at a pre-arranged fee, pay for delivery, and then distribute the pictures in any way he likes. He has bought all rights to the pictures. This arrangement is also possible with the specialized architectural photographer but his normal practice is much more akin to that of the graphic artist; his charges are rated according to the intended use. For most architects and interior designers this is a sensible arrangement. Exclusive use rights are expensive and in any case unnecessary. The designer's primary needs are for office records and display, job presentation, and publication. The fees for these purposes are usually low since residual rights are left with the photographer who can thus get financial return from other sources.

Photographs for advertising are charged on approximately the same basis as the advertising space itself; they are rated according to the size of the space, the circulation of the publication, and the number of times the advertisement is to appear. An architectural photographer may use the same basis for his rate structure for editorial work. Some magazines, in fact, use this basis themselves. Other magazines have established page rates or per photograph rates for editorial matter. Others pay flat assignment fees based on a minimum number of photographs to be taken. Photographer's expenses are paid separately.

Unfortunately, rates for the photography of architecture vary so widely that they are often confusing. Some of the photographer's associations have been attacking this problem but progress is slow so it is necessary for each photographer to learn from others, as well as from editors, the going rate for each publication and then establish his own work's value in relation to quality, experience, and demand. Suffice it to say a top-notch photographer need not worry about his fees for the demand for sensitive interpretive work is great. Payment for an assignment may, on these grounds, vary between $100 and $1,000, and even considerably higher.

This is the general rate structure but there are variants. On assignments most magazines purchase one-time use. This means that the photographer has residual rights and can sell the photograph to other magazines or book publishers after initial publication. For example, a consumer magazine may assign a photographer to do a house. The same photographs may be requested for use by editors of an architectural or building magazine. Because there is no competition between consumer magazines and professional magazines their editors often cooperate in this way on assignments to photographers.

Now there are other aspects to the matter of rights. The designer may assign a photographer to portray his work. Here, too, rates may vary, although most working arrangements with designers are based on a per diem or per photograph charge. A charge of $150, for example, for a day's photography might be established with the assurance of the delivery of a minimum of ten to 15 acceptable photographs. Photographers with more experience and ability might charge $250, or even more, per day, for the delivery of 15 or 20 photographs.

The foregoing fees provide the architect or interior designer with rights to the photographs for office use and exhibit purposes. He may submit them to publications but should first establish an understanding with the photographer as to ownership of editorial rights. Naturally the design firm may acquire full rights. This is particularly prevalent among large firms that have professional public relations representation. Most large architectural and interior design offices disseminate news of their projects through public relations firms. Working with a public relations man is different from working directly with the architect because the former must have completely free use of material. He could not, after all, offer a story to a publication with the condition that the photographs must be paid for by the editor! This means that the purchase of the photographs must be final, with all editorial use rights in the name of the designer or his public relations counsel. The photographer can, and often does, even in this situation, retain the advertising rights. However, this must be clearly defined for advertising representatives of companies often call upon architects and try to get photographs for their use. The understanding must be based on a set fee.

Normally public relations counsel distributes press releases to many media as news stories. The architectural press, however, usually wants an exclusive or at least prior rights on material so for this segment of the press perhaps the best procedure is for the designer to present preliminary data, plans, and renderings of the project as far in advance of completion as possible. These are sent to all publications with an offer for prior rights when the building is completed. An editorial commitment is then possible. The editor may even decide to assign a photographer for a specific slant which assures the architect of getting maximum coverage and leaves him free to use the photographer's work after publication. The fee paid for this latter use is reasonable.

Not all design firms can afford, or even desire, full or part-time public relations services. For such firms the architectural photographer can play a rôle apart from that of photographer. He can provide a liaison between the architect's office and the outside world in his efforts to place photographs with various publications and in various exhibits. He has contacts with architects, interior designers, clients, and magazine and book editors as well as advertising managers of building equipment manufacturers. Sometimes a photographer is even called upon to recommend architects to potential builders. Because of his experience in working with various architects the photographer can be objective in making recommendations.

The photographer who has retained exclusive rights may also distribute the photographs to the manufacturers of products used in the building. If the design is outstanding and the product use unusually attractive, more than one company may wish to utilize the photographs in their advertisements. In such cases the photographer should establish clearly with the designer, on a sound rate structure, the uses intended for the photographs. The details of rights and the mechanics of advertising photography as it pertains to architectural subjects is discussed overleaf.

Besides assignments from designers and advertising agencies, photographers of products are often requested by commercial firms (or their public relations or advertising agencies) for editorial (as opposed to advertising) use in as many magazines as they can be placed with. A fee is paid for the assignment itself but, unless complete rights are purchased, the photographer should make sure that each editorial use is also paid for; a check list of possible uses is a good idea. Fortunately, in such cases, advertising or public relations agencies have budgets for these assignments based upon a carefully calculated formula of space, times used, and media; full rights are usually a part of the transaction.

Book Rights

Of the scores of books published each year on architecture and related subjects most depend a good deal on photog-

The three-dimensional effect of shadows can be used if the right time of day is carefully selected. Residence, Beverly Hills, California. Buff, Straub & Hensman, Architects.

Residence, Los Angeles, California. Frank Lloyd Wright, Architect.

raphy. The acquisition of these photographs, however, is a matter that is not always made crystal clear by the publisher to the prospective author. Often the author seeks illustrations in a hit or miss fashion and for good reason, for the obtaining of photographs from all over the country, or the world, is a complex and confusing task especially when one does not always know what he is seeking. Since there is no clearing house for such material and since the book rights to photographs usually belong to the photographer, the author must track down the material as best he can. The author's manuscript in a typical book contract includes photographs and all other illustrative material. If the author wishes to use 200 photographs he will have quite a bill on his hands for book rights alone. The charge for such photographs may vary from $5 to $500 each and the author, of course, must expect to pay this much. He also must trust that the photographs he tracks down are not of the $500 variety! Actually most photographers who specialize in design work are aware of the need for books and consequently are cooperative in their fees for book use.

Publishers of architectural and design books could smooth the path for their authors by recommending that they get in touch with photographers in various parts of the country. The publisher might even develop a liaison with photographers, learn their operational methods, the extent of their file material, etc. as an aid to his authors. This would make it possible for the author to collect a comprehensive group of illustrations, know the cost in advance, and eliminate a vexatious problem in architectural publishing. Since the photographers would often be able to provide photographs previously published in books and magazines, as well as other unpublished illustrations, it is likely that a large part of the author's requirements would be handled by these contacts alone. It will be evident, too, that considerable time and effort writing to numerous architects and designers would also be eliminated.

Advertising Photography

Photography for advertising is a specialized field that should be discussed here because the architectural photographer is likely to run across it on occasion. If he does it is likely to be concerned with the advertising of building materials, products, and equipment although occasionally a non-bulding item may be involved. An advertiser of building products wants photographs of his product as it appears when installed on a job. The photographer must be sure that his

pictures show not only the product itself but its relationship to the structure in which it is installed. Product photography is a challenge because the art of portraying a product *in situ* requires a sensitive composition to avoid the glamorous close-up which the manufacturer undoubtedly already has by the million. The illustrations (p.134) show a building was photographed for a glass company. Day and night scenes were taken and the building was shown in several moods both in closeups and long shots.

Competition for the eye means that every illustration in an advertising layout must be an eye stopper. As a result more and more companies are improving both the layout and the photography in their advertising. Often the art or photography in an advertising spread is only remotely related to the product concerned.

An architectural photographer, trained in the thinking and vocabulary of the architect, knows what elements of a building will appeal to the designer to whom the advertisement is often aimed. So account executives for building product manufacturers would do well to seek out photographers who are used to photographing architectural subjects for advertising purposes. Conversely, the architectural photographer who is interested in getting into this field might point out this fact to the account executive.

One aspect of advertising photography that causes some difficulty arises because there is so little liaison between the manufacturer and the designer that it is difficult for the former to know when his product has been specified in a way that would be desirable for advertising purposes. Even if the manufacturer knew that his glass (say) was used effectively in a building it would be hard for him to be certain it was indeed his product that was used and not a competitive product that was substituted for it under the ''or equal'' clause of the specifications. In the case of such products as glass only the supplier can determine whether brand A or brand B was used because many suppliers carry more than one brand.

One possible method for getting around these difficulties as far as advertising photography is concerned was worked out by the author for the G. M. Basford Company, advertising representatives for American St. Gobain Glass Company. It is distributed to salesmen and jobbers of their products. Thus, if a large sale were made, say, in Ames, Iowa for a new dormitory at Iowa State University and the representative felt this building were of sufficient interest to be

A thin, reinforced, corrugated concrete shell forms the roof and two walls of the ice skating rink. The interior picture has been taken in natural light at f/22, 1/50th seconds. Ice Rink, Encino, California. Carl L. Maston, Architect.

Autumn tones and a park-like landscape created an almost ideal setting for a glass in architecture advertising assignment. The use of infra-red film in the lower picture has completely changed the mood. Photographing the product in its setting makes for a more informative picture. Washington Water & Power Co., Spokane, Washington. Kenneth Brooks and Bruce Walker, Architects. Larry Halpern, Landscape Architect. Courtesy G. M. Basford Co. & American St. Gobain Glass Co.

132

used in advertising, he could, by filling in the following check list, bring it up for consideration. If the client and agency feel it is worth pursuing they can send a photographer out for complete pictorial coverage.

Subject: Check list for American St. Gobain architectural representatives and jobbers for reporting projects for possible photography.

1. Send snapshots, preferably Polaroid, taken when building is *complete*. This means with landscaping finished and the grounds clear of all debris.

2. Check out all American St. Gobain glass on the job. This must be authentic so the jobber has to be interviewed and the glass double checked on the job.

3. A list of the types of glass and their location on the building to be prepared.

4. Proper authorities should be approached before the snapshots are sent so as to verify permission to use material on the building for advertising and promotion. This should include permission to take interior and exterior photographs, day and night. Some buildings may have to be done on weekends so clearance is to be arranged for this. Names of proper authorities to be contacted in the event the building is chosen for photography to be sent with snapshots.

5. A plan of the building with compass points marked will help in the selection of the best time of day for sun angles.

6. There is no use in reporting non-photogenic buildings; for example, glass walls covered with louvers will surely not do anything for the glass hidden from view! The design of the building should have architectural significance. Avoid tricky cliches.

7. All names associated with the project to be assembled: architect, interior designer, landscape architect, general contractor, subcontractors, jobbers, and suppliers.

The problem of tracing a product and making sure that it had actually been used on a job would be eased considerably if there were some industry-wide method of identification. A plaque listing the products used in a building would make it simpler for advertisers, photographers, and anyone else who might be interested to learn what products were used on the job. Often the first view the general public gets of new products or new ideas on the uses of familiar products, for example, is in public and commercial buildings. If they find them attractive it would be easy, in this way, to discover by whom they were manufactured and supplied. Alternatively, the individual manufacturer could use an unobtrusive logo-

The following series of pictures was taken on a glass advertising assignment, the advertisements to be used in building magazines. The form and moods of the structure have been expressed under all types of lighting and weather conditions. Federal Building, Sacramento, California. Courtesy of G. M. Basford Company and American St. Gobain Glass Company.

Careful attention to structure in atmospheric moods in essential. Below is a "straight" photograph; opposite is the same view with the camera corrected to restore more normal perspective and with infra-red film. The time of day was also different and the light in the second photograph is cloud-diffused.

The same side of the building as before but from the normal commercial elevation view.

Taken at twilight in the rain with the camera protected by the parking garage structure. A 75 mm extreme wide angle lens was used to get between the columns of the parking structure.

Taken the next morning from the roof of the parking structure and a slightly different angle. A 90 mm wide angle lens was used; the north-facing facade required particularly careful exposure.

This dramatic protruding form was not clearly evident in the two previous scenes and therefore required separate attention.

This detail of the entrance was taken at early twilight in the rain with a 127 mm lens.

After the storm the rain-soaked street could be exploited for an intriguing photograph.

type on his own product. So far as the photographer is concerned, some such identification system might save him a long trip to photograph an installation that was reported by the company's local representative on information from the supplier as being brand A only to discover that brand B had been substituted at the last minute.

One more thing should be said about advertising photography. Architects and other designers are rarely credited in advertisements whereas photographers frequently are. This is embarrassing because (a) it is the designer who specified the product in the first place and (b) the advertisement usually appears in publications aimed at and read by designers anyway. The reasons given by advertising companies for this curious situation are merely weak alibis blaming "policy." The photographer, who holds the rights on a photograph, should release it only on the firm condition that design credits be given when it is published.

Studio and Office

Compared to the needs of the portrait and commercial photographer, the architectural photographer has simple physical plant requirements. With little or no traffic to his mousetrap, he is not concerned with a studio front. His main concern is that his office be in good running order and that it have an efficient system of filing and record keeping.

A record book, similar to a log, and starting with job number 1 should be instituted. In it would be listed the names of architects, interior designers, their clients, their projects, and the locations and dates of each! A file of negatives with job numbers corresponding to the log book and a similar file of contact prints is also necessary. Contact prints are essential for reference for they are marked with cropping lines and various instructions for enlarging.

There should be a file of 8 x 10 prints but it must be kept up-to-date to avoid clutter. On jobs that are not likely to be re-ordered, 8 x 10's are unnecessary but prints should be kept on hand for fast service on jobs where re-orders and stock photograph requests are frequent. Such re-orders will start when the photographer's work begins to appear in publications.

All jobs should be classified in a crossfile as they are completed. Such a reference system indicates exactly what photographs are on file. For example, if the ceiling of a new and architecturally unusual bowling alley uses brand A acoustic

tile, it should be crossfiled under the category "ceiling tile." Then if a request comes from the manufacturer, a quick flip of the file will indicate what material is available. Likewise, during slow periods, product photographs can be sent for possible use to advertisers along with a view of the exterior of the building to show the nature of the design.

A record of all transactions should be kept, preferably in the master log, so that the history of any project is visible at a glance.

To provide up-to-the-minute efficiency, a secretary should be employed although, of course, in the beginning it is often necessary for all the jobs to be done by one person. Perhaps the darkroom assistant could provide the secretarial help until the work load can support a full time secretary. When the secretary does enter the scene she can be trained to perform other duties such as print drying and dispatching orders.

The darkroom procedure must be simplified so that rapid, efficient service is the rule thus insuring maximum return for time spent in the field. Ideally the darkroom should be run by an assistant. Many photographers can readily employ a top grade darkroom technician but refuse to do so on the grounds that they could never find anyone good enough. This attitude is unrealistic because with a short period of indoctrination any experienced darkroom man can be instructed to produce quality prints of architectural subjects.

One of the greatest problems confronting the photographic profession is a lack of business judgment. Photographers are likely to feel they can take the photographs, return to the darkroom, process the negatives, make prints, and then deliver the prints all alone. They may be overlooking the fact that time spent in the darkroom is wasted so far as field work is concerned, and it is the field work which is basic; it is the one area for which the photographer himself is best fitted. To obtain adequate returns for this field work his time should not be spent doing work which could be farmed out. He can rarely charge enough to cover adequately a day's shooting plus the time spent in the darkroom and in assembling orders. In addition, efficiency is likely to suffer because of the inevitable delays brought about when field assignments prevent the photographer attending to his darkroom work. This may seem elementary but scores of photographers still work in this obsolete fashion.

Many photographers, even busy profession magazine workers, utilize the services of laboratories which specialize in high quality processing of negatives and prints. This kind of service is worth looking into for it will permit the beginner to devote all of his time to assignments. This method of processing insures delivery of the work on schedule. While charges for outside processing may seem high in proportion to his income, simple arithmetic will demonstrate that it will more than pay for itself within a short time.

Another consideration the photographer must settle are working arrangements for the photography, and publicity, of a building. It is not uncommon to find the following people involved in the program: the architect, the interior designer, the landscape architect, the contractors, and the manufacturers of materials and equipment. Obviously, if each of these interested parties employs his own photographers, the result would be bedlam, particularly if tenants were moving in at the same time the photographs were being taken. There is also likely to be such a proliferation of publicity programs that no single party benefits fully. Therefore, before a building is completed some liaison must be established among all the parties concerned making it possible to organize the photography and publicity efficiently; this also involves general agreement as to how the photographs are to be used. This is not so complicated as it sounds.

Most of the parties concerned are, after all, anxious to get the greatest possible benefit on their promotional effort and if cooperation will help achieve this they will be willing to work together. The best way to accomplish this may be through the architect and his photographer. Between them they can probably furnish good advice and good photographic coverage. In most cases a set of photographs can best be taken by one photographer who can move in with his equipment once and work right through the project so that no area is omitted. Thus all the photographic work is completed at one time, confusion of photographs is avoided, and the tenant is not interrupted constantly by a stream of photographers during his first few months when confusion is likely to be rife anyway.

In addition to his work for architects or other people directly concerned with a building, the photographer may receive assignments directly from magazines. This type of work has great appeal to the creative photographer for it involves some of the best current architecture and requires the best photographic quality a photographer can achieve and a modicum of editorial work in the photographing of the structure concerned. Needless to say, this area of work requires long, hard effort before enough experience is gained to bring requests from magazines. The magazines which give such assignments include the professional architectural magazines, home service magazines, house organs, technical trade journals, and some women's or general circulation magazines which periodically publish stories and reports on architecture and interiors. The preference of the editors for assigning their own photographer rather than going directly to the architect is understandable. The magazines use photographers they know they can rely on and thereby eliminate the long negotiations with architects and other design sources which are sometimes required to obtain the exact kind of photographic material they like to publish.

Perhaps the most significant advice that can be given is to complete assignments and delivery of photographs with dispatch for others often depend on the photographer's output.

Just as mounted enlargements enhance architect's offices, so can they provide atmosphere in a photographer's work or display rooms. A standard salon size print, 16 x 20, should be used. This is ideal for visual impact. It is also easy to carry so it serves a dual purpose for it acts as an incentive to hold exhibits and participate in competitions. Many public agencies will hang exhibits of the architectural photographer's work because it attracts many viewers. Photographers can also coordinate exhibit activities with architects' offices and help in their preparation.

Another invaluable tool to the photographer is a plastic binding machine which consists of a punch and a binding unit. With such a machine the photographer can easily assemble handsome bound books for presentation purposes.

In conclusion, I might say what is probably evident throughout the text and the illustration of this book. I enjoy photography, I like architects and editors. I hope these people will find this book valuable and I hope, too, that it may inspire young photographers to tread the path that has made the past twenty-five years of my life—which is the length of my career as an architectural photographer—challenging and rewarding. Every man must make his contribution to society. The architectural photographer makes his by helping to improve the physical environment of his community.

Acknowledgements and Bibliography

I met Richard Neutra after I took my first photographs of a modern building early in 1936. The building was a house he had designed and which I was visiting. In quick succession thereafter I met Raphael Soriano, who was doing his first house, Gregory Ain, who was already well-known, and the late R. M. Schindler, who impressed me with his brilliance and daring even in those days when I was so innocent of the world of architecture. Harwell Hamilton Harris and J. R. Davidson also had done some of their best work by this time. I wish first, then, to acknowledge my debt to them and to express gratitude for their patience. Their teaching enabled me to develop an understanding of design concepts and philosophies. It was a great privilege to have been in the company of these modern architectural pioneers and giants. My thanks also to the many architects and designers who have helped me since then.

The late Julius Frank, who was for many years a faithful and devoted darkroom assistant, deserves a special word of thanks as does his wife, Hildegarde, who upon his untimely death stepped in and continued the work; all of the prints used to publish this book were, in fact, made by Hildegarde Frank. I also wish to express my appreciation to Mrs. Esther G. Roe, my secretary, for her participation over several years in the writing and preparation of this manuscript. The book would not have been possible, either, without the close co-operation of the editors of the Whitney Library of Design.

In place of a formal bibliography I want to recommend a couple of books which I think are particularly useful to those who wish to find out more about photography in general. They are:

Eye, Film, and Camera in Color Photography by Ralph M. Evans. John Wiley & Sons, New York.

Corrective Photography by Lewis L. Kellsey. An elementary illustrated text on camera swings and how to use them. Deardorff, Chicago.

I also recommend the numerous data publications of the Eastman Kodak Company which are sold in most camera stores and carry excellent and thorough information on all facets of photography. The would-be photographer is advised to visit his library as often as possible for he will find scores of books on the theory and practice of photography there. The Evans book mentioned above is not only one of the finest treatises on color theory written to date but it also contains first-rate discussions on the elements of optics, vision, composition, lighting, chemistry, and camera use.

Finally I want to say that without the help and companionship of my wife, Emma, neither this book nor the career upon which it is based would have been possible.

J. S.

List of Illustrations

Index